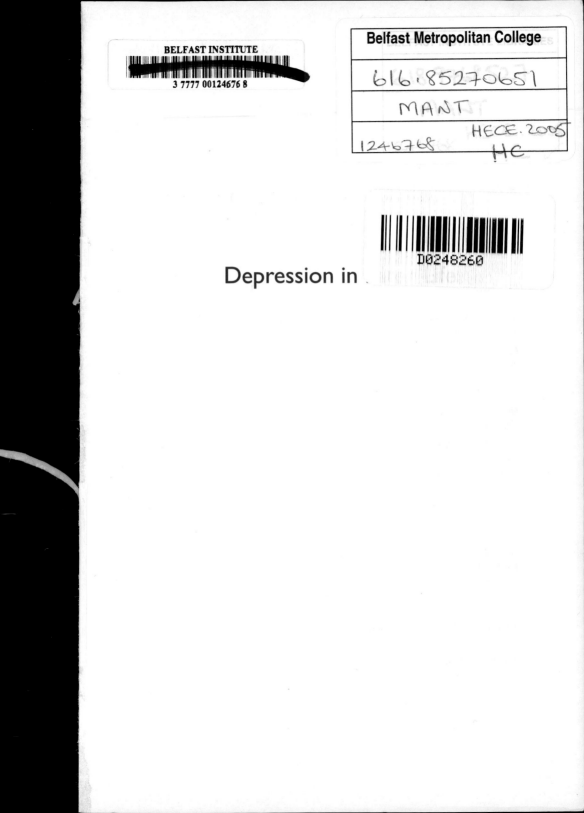

D0248260

Depression in

also by Jill Manthorpe

Students' Mental Health Needs
Problems and Responses
Edited by Nicky Stanley and Jill Manthorpe
ISBN 1 85302 983 1

also by Steve Iliffe

Primary Care and Dementia
Steve Iliffe and Vari Drennan
ISBN 1 85302 997 1

of related interest

The Simplicity of Dementia
A Guide for Family and Carers
Huub Buijssen
ISBN 1 84310 321 4

Dancing with Dementia
My Story of Living Positively with Dementia
Christine Bryden
ISBN 1 84310 332 X

Spiritual Care in Later Life
Elizabeth MacKinlay
ISBN 1 84310 231 5

Past Trauma in Late Life
European Perspectives on Therapeutic Work with
Older People
Edited by Linda Hunt, Mary Marshall and Cherry Rowlings
ISBN 1 85302 446 5

The Psychology of Ageing
An Introduction, 3rd Edition
Ian Stuart-Hamilton
ISBN 1 85302 771 5

Depression in Later Life

Jill Manthorpe and Steve Iliffe

Jessica Kingsley Publishers
London and Philadelphia

First published in 2005
by Jessica Kingsley Publishers
116 Pentonville Road
London N1 9JB, UK
and
400 Market Street, Suite 400
Philadelphia, PA 19106, USA

www.jkp.com

Library of Congress Cataloging in Publication Data
Manthorpe, Jill, 1955-
   Depression in later life / Jill Manthorpe and Steve Iliffe.
   p. cm.
   Includes bibliographical references and index.
   ISBN-13: 978-1-84310-234-2 (pbk. : alk. paper)
   ISBN-10: 1-84310-234-X (pbk. : alk. paper) 1. Geriatric psychiatry. 2. Depression, Mental.
3. Older people--Mental health. I. Iliffe, Steve. II. Title.
   RC451.4.A5M35 2005
   618.97'689--dc22

                          2005008299

British Library Cataloguing in Publication Data
A CIP catalogue record for this book is available from the British Library

ISBN-13: 978 1 84310 234 2
ISBN-10: 1 84310 234 X

Printed and Bound in Great Britain by
Athenaeum Press, Gateshead, Tyne and Wear

Contents

Contents

CHAPTER I

Why Focus on Depression?

Depression is the commonest mental health problem in later life. At least one in ten people aged 65 or more have significant symptoms of depression like sadness, loss of energy and difficulties sleeping (Sharma and Copeland 1989). Those with illness or disabilities that limit their capability to deal with the tasks of everyday life, or who depend on others for a great deal of help, are more likely to be depressed than those who are more independent or less burdened with ill-health. Older people visiting their general practitioner (GP) are particularly likely to be experiencing depression symptoms, particularly the 'physical' symptoms of depression like persistent fatigue, headaches or widespread muscular aches and pains, or poor concentration and memory, and these symptoms may not be recognized for what they are (Lyness *et al.* 1999; Olafsdottir, Marcusson and Skoog 2001; Watts *et al.* 2002). People who are housebound are twice as likely to experience depression than more mobile older people, perhaps not surprisingly (Bruce and McNamara 1992). People living in sheltered accommodation are even more likely to experience depression, with closer to one in four individuals reporting depressive symptoms (Field, Walker and Orrell 2002). High rates of depression are found among users of home care services (Patmore 2002). Poverty and depression seem to go together, and poorer and less educated older people show less awareness of the symptoms

7

of depression and are less likely to seek help or treatment. Depression is more common in older women than in older men.

In this book we are going to use both medical and psychosocial models of depression, because both are useful. In the medical model patterns of symptoms are grouped together to make diagnoses, and these can guide professionals and patients alike towards optimal treatments. The medical model concentrates on brain biochemistry, and seeks to alter it in the depressed person. Social and psychological models of depression are equally helpful because they can enable us to make sense of the complexity of depression. Psychosocial perspectives focus on the ways people learn to deal with adversity (the development of coping strategies), or on the ways that negative thinking affects behaviour, or on the effects of social relationships on mood and psychological well-being. A 'social model' looks in particular at social causes of depression but, as Golightly (2004) points out, medical and social models only get separated in academic or research thinking, far less so in practice where most practitioners take both perspectives on board. One of the main emphases of a social model approach is that it looks at how factors interact to enhance vulnerability and this is particularly relevant to older people whose histories are long and whose circumstances are often changing. Golightly (2004) summarizes the central points of a social model as, first, the taking into account of individual predisposing factors, for example, our genes, our family, our life history; second, social causes such as living in poverty; and third, psychological factors such as loss, threat, highly critical relationships, a lack of resilience and limited networks of support.

All of us have experienced sadness, and many of us have experienced depression, but it is not always easy to tell the difference, either when you are experiencing these mood changes yourself or when observing someone else. How can we distinguish between depression and understandable sadness in a practical way? Using a medical approach to understanding the experiences of depression, we suggest the following three rules of thumb, *all* of which must apply:

- *Duration*: Symptoms of depression (we discuss these in detail later) are present for at least two weeks. This time limit is, of course, somewhat arbitrary, but it does seem to be a cut-off point for the kinds of sadness that are triggered by normal life events like losses, illness and failure.

- *Lack of fluctuation*: Symptoms of depression occur on most days, most of the time. Other events do not distract the person, and 'good days' (or even periods of the day) are few.

- *Intensity*: The severity of depression symptoms must be of a degree that is definitely not normal for that individual, so that they say 'I have never felt this bad before', or describe tiredness more profound than usual in a busy life, sleeplessness more frequent and prolonged than in the past, and so on.

These rules of thumb help to separate understandable sadness from depression, but they do not tell you which *symptoms* are the key signs of depression, and which are possible but not diagnostic. In this medical model the key symptoms of depression are as shown in Box 1.1.

Other symptoms that suggest depression include:

- suicidal thoughts or behaviour

- loss of confidence or self-esteem

- feeling of helplessness

- inappropriate or excessive feelings of guilt

- feelings of hopelessness or worthlessness

- avoiding social contacts or going out

- poor concentration and/or difficulty with memory

- physical slowing or agitation (restlessness or fidgeting)
- sleep disturbance (particularly waking in the early hours and not being able to return to sleep)
- reduced appetite with corresponding weight loss.

Box 1.1 Key symptoms of depression
(Alexopoulos et al. 2001)

An individual has depression if any of the following three criteria apply:

1. They have a depressed mood sustained for at least two weeks (on most days, much of the time).

and/or

2. They have lost interest or pleasure in usual activities (in medical jargon, 'anhedonia').

and/or

3. They report decreased energy, increased fatigue (in people who are physically ill this may mean feelings of fatigue even when not attempting exertion), or diminished activity.

We will return to the advantages of the medical model of depression later, but first want to mention some of its disadvantages. While treatments derived from a medical model work for some older people with depression, they do not work for all, and even when they relieve the symptoms there can be a high risk of relapse. And, to make the situation more complicated, doctors and nurses may not always use the medical model, with its rules about patterns of symptoms. This can be a practical problem in working with older people, in two ways. Expectations of 'cure' can be raised in discussing with someone why they should seek help for their depression, only to be disappointed when treatments have little or no effect. Similarly, a lot of effort and negotiation can go into persuading a reluctant older person to describe his or her feelings and symptoms to a doctor, only to find that the doctor does not recognize the problem as depression at all. It is important to understand how these problems arise, and what can be done about them. We will return to the effectiveness of different treatments again, both in this chapter and in Chapter 3, but first want to explore the problem of recognition further.

As a whole it seems true to say that depression in later life is under-diagnosed and under-treated. Studies of older people living at home show consistent under-documentation of depression in medical records when these are compared with the known burden of depression in the wider population (Garrard, Rolnick and Nitz 1998). Only a small minority of depressed older individuals with significant symptoms receive treatment or referral for specialist care, even when their general practitioners recognize their depressed state (MacDonald 1986). The severity of the depression and high levels of anxiety expressed by the older person seem to be triggers for referral (Eustace *et al.* 2001). Both general practitioners and hospital doctors have been criticised for their tendency to miss depression in their patients (Audit Commission 2000) but as we shall see the manifestation and patterns of depression in older people in the community are so complex, and the uncertainties about the effectiveness of intervention are so great, that under-diagnosis is inevitable. Depressed people may think of themselves as weak if they admit to depression, and see it as a stigmatizing description to be avoided, and their perspective may divert attention from the mental health problem to physical explanations. Professionals may find themselves focusing on the headache, sleeplessness, back pain or other symptoms described by the depressed older person, or on a request for vitamins or a tonic, rather than thinking about underlying, but perhaps well hidden, disturbances of thinking and emotion.

Professionals and older people themselves underestimate the significance of late life depression despite evidence that:

- late life depression is associated with disproportionately high rates of suicide and high death rates from all other medical causes (Montano 1999)

- depression in later life is associated with high use of both medical and social services (Beekman *et al.* 1997) and depressed older people are more likely to be treated for anxiety (or physical symptoms like pain) than with anti-depressants or psychological therapies

- depression particularly affects those older people caring for others.

Not all of those older people whose depression is diagnosed are treated appropriately (with anti-depressants or psychological therapies), but they are likely to be treated for anxiety or physical symptoms like pain, which may be the surface manifestations of the underlying depressive disorder. Since the commonest drugs used for suicide by self-poisoning among older people are Paracetamol and Paracetamol-based compounds like Co-proxamol (Distalgesic), treatment of symptoms rather than causes can be hazardous, and caution is recommended in their use if an older person is depressed (Shah, Uren and Baker 2002). We will return to the risk of suicide in Chapter 6, and only mention it here to emphasize the importance of thinking beyond the surface pattern of symptoms in an older person to seek their cause, just as in any physical disorder or trouble affecting quality of life. The first practice example of Mr A illustrates how a diagnosis of depression could be missed because symptoms are misattributed to other causes, or the older person wants to avoid the diagnosis itself.

The general practitioner who sees Mr A does need to think about physical illnesses that might cause Mr A's symptoms and should investigate to rule them out, but he or she should not lose sight of the possibility that Mr A is developing a serious depressive illness. Apart from his reluctance to consider depression, diagnosis in Mr A's case may be relatively straightforward, but it is often not so clear-cut. The features of the encounter

Practice example: Mr A, aged 76

Mr A rarely visits his GP, but goes to the medical centre one day complaining that he has no energy, and is sleeping badly. He wakes frequently at night and feels weary when he gets up in the morning. He has lost his appetite. His wife died three years ago following a stroke. While he volunteers that he does not get out and enjoy himself these days he is adamant that he is not depressed. He wants a 'tonic'.

Learning points

Note the typical symptoms of, and the possible trigger factor (bereavement) for depression. Like many of his generation Mr A does not want a stigmatizing psychiatric label.

Depression is more likely to be the cause of his symptoms and experiences than are physical illnesses, although it is important to make sure that he does not have iron or vitamin B12 deficiency, or diabetes.

We need to know what his previous ('pre-morbid') personality was like. How has he coped with adverse events before? As we shall see in Chapter 3, if he has not previously experienced depression the impact of anti-depressant treatment may be more limited. In any case, social support may be more important than medical intervention. The first task in responding to Mr A may be to get another person's perspective on how he has changed.

between the older person and their doctor (or nurse, social worker or family member) that might wrongly reduce the suspicion of depression are:

- high levels of anxiety without other immediately obvious depression symptoms. If Mr A shows only anxiety, he may be offered treatments for it that fail to address his probable depression

- a disability that makes depression seem appropriate, with the other person thinking 'I would be depressed in your position'

- a long history of depressed periods occurring so frequently that depression seems normal for the person (it may be, in some senses, but this does not mean that it is not serious in an older person)

- a recent loss that makes the depression understandable (again, this may be partially true, in that losses can trigger depression, but that is no reason to underestimate the significance of the symptoms)

- multiple and confusing physical symptoms, like aches and pains that migrate from place to place, and that are difficult to match with any known physical illness

- a very obvious problem of memory loss, confusion or poor concentration

- resistance to the idea of depression from the older person or the family

- a limited impact of the depression on others (a depressed older person may be quiet, even apathetic, and so easier to be with and look after)

From this list there are four very important clinical problems that those working with older people in social work, nursing, medicine and allied health professions need to understand when trying to unravel complicated patterns of symptoms: anxiety, disability, somatization and dementia.

Anxiety

Anxiety is common, to some extent normal and in some situations entirely appropriate. We devote Chapter 5 to it, but there are some basic issues about anxiety that have to be understood, to get depression in perspective. Many psychiatrists have argued that anxiety symptoms are the visible face of depression, and that in later life anxiety is depression until proved otherwise. This may be an over-simplification, but it does capture the way in which anxiety symptoms can be layered onto depression, confusing the person experiencing them as much as they mislead those around the depressed individual. As we get older we are less likely to develop anxiety symptoms for the first time, although the number of older people with such symptoms at any moment in time remains substantial (Weiss 1996). Up to 1 in 10 older people living at home have symptoms of persistent anxiety (Flint 1994). A third of older people visiting their general practitioner have 'generalized' anxiety – multiple symptoms set off by lots of situations (Krasucki *et al.* 1999). 'Phobic' anxiety, with symptoms triggered by specific situations or settings – encountering spiders, travelling by bus, mixing with others – is also common, affecting between 5 per cent and 10 per cent of people aged 65 and over, particularly older women (Kramer, German and Anthony 1985). In the absence of disabling physical problems phobic anxiety may be the underlying cause of individuals becoming housebound in 20 per cent of cases (Exton Smith, Stanton and Windsor 1976), while recurrence of post-traumatic stress disorder may become a problem for veterans of war (Floyd, Rice and Black 2002) or similar exposure to violence. Anxiety symptoms are the commonest mental health problem associated with depression (Blanchard, Waterrus and Mann 1994), and the majority of older people identified as having generalized anxiety disorder (GAD) also have depression symptoms (Lindesay, Briggs and Murphy 1989). A third of depressed older people have had at least one lifetime anxiety disorder diagnosis, and this is associated with poorer social function and a high level of physical symptoms (Lenze, Mulsant and Shear 2000).

However, anxiety symptoms are also part of normal experience, as part of a healthy and necessary 'fight or flight' reaction to danger, and are by no means inappropriate or a sign of mental ill-health. The older person being bullied, abused or exploited by others has every reason to be anxious, and should not be too speedily categorized as mentally ill. Likewise persistent anxiety symptoms should not be attributed instantly to frailty, prolonged disability, 'a nervous disposition' or similar explanations that fail to make strong connections between causes and effects. Professionals therefore walk 'a fine line between pathologising a healthy response and failing to recognise neurotic dysfunction' (Beinfeld *et al.* 1994). In practice this is not always an easy issue to unravel, even for experienced practitioners, and so we will return to explore the problem of anxiety overlapping with depression further in Chapter 5.

Disability and depression

Depression and disability commonly go together but most older people with disabilities are not depressed. Explanations about associations between disabilities, illness and depression symptoms that simply show the overlap statistically are not satisfactory, because disability and depression can cause each other, and increased disability due to depression is only partly explained by personal characteristics like age, sex, ethnicity, social class or education, or by medical conditions and cognitive ability (Lenze, Rogers 2001). Here we run out of strong evidence, largely because of the shortage of long-term studies of depression in the community (Katona 1989). The association between poor health and depression appears to be stronger for men and for those aged 75 and over than for women and 'younger' old people (aged 65–74 years). Poor health, loss of mobility and depression are linked with loneliness and social isolation (Cattan 2002). Subjective measures of ill-health like pain, or self-rating of overall healthiness and well-being, are more strongly related to depression than are more objective measures of illness or disability like the number of chronic diseases or the degree of functional limitation (Beekman, Kriegsman and Deeg 1995). Nearly a third of

---

Practice example: Mrs B, aged 81

Mrs B has emphysema (a long-term lung disease) and type 2 diabetes (the type treated with diet and tablets, not insulin injections). Recently she learned that she has a cataract in one eye, after noticing a change in her vision. She gets very short of breath when walking, even on the flat, and stairs are becoming a major problem for her. Her husband died ten years ago, and her only son died from a brain tumour at the age of 35. She has started cooking classes at the local college, and has one or two friends whom she sees each month. She visits her doctor regularly with lots of vague aches and pains, saying she has 'no get up and go' and that she has 'lived too long'.

Learning points

Disability and depression are linked, with disability provoking bereavement in relation to the loss of the able self. Depression impairs functioning, creating a 'chicken and egg' situation – in this case the physical problems are profound, and their amelioration may be an effective anti-depressant. Somatization can be an acceptable way of dealing with distress, and reducing it may not be the best option, but it needs *containment,* by which we mean attentiveness to the individual's concerns without collusion with the beliefs attached to symptoms.

---

older people with four or more medical problems are depressed, compared with 1 in 20 of those without a significant illness (Kennedy, Kelman and Thomas 1990), and the frequency of depression among patients with poor physical health attending their general practitioner is twice that of healthy older people (Evans and Katona 1993).

Physical symptoms and 'somatization'

Making sense of physical symptoms and teasing out physical illness from depression are not necessarily easy. When are people ill, and when do they show depressive 'somatization' or a 'somatization disorder'? To answer this we need to focus on the somatization process, and understand that somatization has four components:

1. seeking help for physical (somatic) manifestations of a psychiatric disorder

2. attribution of bodily symptoms to physical rather than emotional or psychological disturbance

3. a detectable psychiatric condition, using standard diagnostic criteria like those found in the National Institute for Clinical Excellence guidelines

4. relief of the somatic complaints (or their return to earlier levels) through treatment of the psychiatric disorder.

(Craig and Boardman 1990)

Somatization is common in depressed older people, especially in those with physical illness, as the example of Mrs B on page 17 illustrates. Psychological distress is not usually masked, but the best way to help these individuals is often unclear (Sheehan and Banerjee 1999). In principle, the aim is to re-attribute the symptom to psychological causes, and away from physical explanations. This requires a lot of skill, and is a reason for involving a clinical psychologist or community mental health nurse in supporting the depressed individual – provided there is consent.

Depression and dementia

Depression is more common than dementia, except among the very old (those aged 85 or more) but is not so visible to health and social care staff because it causes less dependency, and is not a cause for relocation to a care home. However, dementia may begin with depression symptoms, particularly if the person with dementia becomes aware of his or her changing memory and mental capacity. Distinguishing between depression and dementia is not always easy, and so we will return to this problem in Chapter 4.

Types of depression

The term 'depression' now means so many different things to so many different people that it may be losing its use as a description of an understandable mental health problem. The medical model recognizes this, indirectly, and so divides depression into different sub-categories, sometimes with new names that appear to be attempts to escape from the vague and confusing 'depression' label. We are going to concentrate on four main categories: major depression, so-called minor depression, chronic depression and short-term adjustment disorders. Figure 1.1 shows these categories as they emerge at the ends of the branches of a diagnostic decision tree. The different branches are distinguished by the severity and duration of symptoms, and as we shall see in Chapter 3, the categorization helps to decide how best to support and treat the depressed individual.

This logic pathway is easier to follow than it seems at first sight. If the symptoms of depression have been present for at least two weeks, and more than five (from the lists above), you are carried down the left side of the decision path towards major depression or an 'organic mood disorder' – a change in brain function brought on by illness, legal or illegal drugs, or alcohol in excess. If there are fewer than five symptoms you are taken down the right side of the decision path, towards types of depression that are different in their duration, from brief depressive episodes to dysthymia, that lasts years. These different categories of depression are explained in the next section of this chapter.

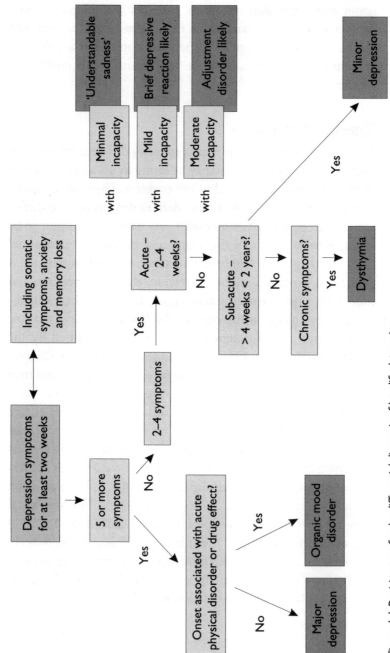

Figure 1.1 Decision tree for the differential diagnosis of late life depression

Major depression

Only a minority of those with depressive symptoms have sufficient symptoms, of sufficient severity, to warrant the diagnosis of major depression, but this is the group of older people for whom anti-depressant therapy is most effective. Of course the boundary between major depression and other types is blurred, and the category depends on a subjective judgement. Nonetheless, if you feel that an older person is severely affected by multiple symptoms of depression, seeking medical help from the person's GP is appropriate, even contacting the out-of-hours service if you fear a suicide risk. Most older people have fewer depression symptoms and fall into the categories of adjustment reaction, 'minor depression' or chronic depression. In all of these categories older people and their families may contest the appropriateness of the label of depression. In some cultures there may be problems in using the term if it is not recognized, or if it is called a feeling of sorrow, anxiety or burden (Beliappa 1991, p.2). It is also the case that too little is known about the effectiveness of treatments for these types of depression with fewer symptoms, and therefore they are the most problematic to deal with in social care, nursing or general practice.

Minor depression

This is the form of depression in later life that is characterized by variability of symptoms (and sometimes the dominance of anxiety), somatization, and an association with disability. It has acquired many names – 'demoralization syndrome', 'dysphoria', 'atypical depression', 'masked depression', 'sub-syndromal depression' among others (Gallo, Rabins and Iliffe 1997). The characteristics of minor depression are shown in Box 1.2. In studies of older people living at home it is about three times more common than major depression and is therefore the most common type of depression encountered in primary care (Heun, Papassotiropoulos and Ptok 2000).

Box 1.2 *'Minor depression'*

'Minor depression' in the community is:

- found amongst older people with worse illness
- associated with functional impairment, which may wax and wane in synchrony with depressive symptoms
- associated with cognitive impairment
- linked to later major depression, as a possible precursor state
- associated with social and family impairment
- associated with higher death rates from all causes.

Chronic depression – 'dysthymia'

Dysthymia, in the sense of a long-lasting depressive state, goes together with significant physical impairment (Kirby, Bruce *et al.* 1999). One complex study of a large group of older people with physical disabilities found that worsening of disabilities had a strong and immediate effect on depressive symptoms, making them worse, followed by a delayed but less powerful effect of depression on disability, making it worse about a year later (Ormel *et al.* 2002). We can speculate about three ways in which depression and disability are related:

1. Depression is a clear reaction to illness or disability, or its treatment, which fluctuates with the severity of the illness. For example, depression commonly develops after a person has survived a stroke.

2. Depression precedes the illness or disability, but shares an origin with it (e.g. a life event like bereavement). Bereavement increases the risks of illness and death in the bereaved person, particularly from heart disease.

3. Depression can precede the onset of the physical problems and may be responsible for them (a somatization disorder). An example of this is the way that depression amplifies pain caused by physical disorders like arthritis.

(Mofic and Paykel 1975)

Adjustment disorders

The types of depression that are obviously triggered by an important life event but that go on slightly longer than expected are on the border between minor depression and understandable sadness. Someone who takes longer than expected to recover psychologically from a loss, or a serious illness, may fall into this category, and the key implication for the practitioner in any discipline who encounters such disorders is to work out whether recovery from the depressed state is happening or not.

The implications of these different categories and descriptions are potentially serious. Major depression needs to be identified, and medical or psychological treatments offered for it, because its consequences are so great (see Chapter 2). Minor depression is less easy to treat, but in a minority of individuals seems to develop into major depression, so it needs to be taken seriously. Chronic depression is less amenable to change, so support strategies are needed for its containment and management. Adjustment reactions are less of a problem because they do resolve, in time, and all that may be required from care home staff or practitioners working in the community is short-term support.

This chapter has introduced some of the main themes of this book. We have outlined that depression is common and complex, and associated with a variety of losses. Depression can be disguised by anxiety, hidden behind physical symptoms and complaints, and confused with early dementia. Depression is different from normal sadness – it is more intense, less variable and lasts longer. Telling the difference between a normal adjustment to an event and an 'adjustment disorder' is often difficult. There are discernable types of depression – severe (major depression), long-lasting but less intense (minor depression), or very long- lasting and associated with disabilities (dysthymia). The impact of depression is also variable and we explore this in the following chapter.

CHAPTER 2

The Impact of Depression

Because depression has so many different symptoms and because it can take so many different forms in each episode or over the years, it is sometimes hard to think about its impact. We can measure it objectively as one of the world's major disabilities causing massive social and economic damage, and we can sympathize subjectively with the highly personal experiences that a depressed person will go through. We think it is important to consider the multiple layers of impact because this can assist us to respond appropriately and effectively. If we do not understand the impact of depression on the person, on those with whom they are in contact and on the wider community then we may not listen closely enough to the people involved, and so miss cues about the severity of depression, and find it hard to assess the extent of recovery. As we shall discuss in more detail in the next chapter, where we outline the help that is available, support for people with depression needs to be tailored to their circumstances, beliefs and coping resources. These too affect the impact of depression upon them.

This chapter looks at four linked but discrete areas of depression's impact. We start with the impact on the older person, look at the impact on family and friends, then on other social networks, and finally turn to practitioners supporting or in contact with the older person. Carers' needs and resources are covered in particular detail in Chapter 7.

The impact on the person

What does it feel like to have depression? It may be helpful to think about the symptoms we described in Chapter 1 and what it feels like to experience them. Autobiographical accounts of depression, like that from Wolpert (1999), provide some clues, as do other personal accounts available from mental health support groups such as those linked to the Depression Alliance. Writers such as Styron (1996) describe the sudden onset of depression in later life (in his case when aged 60) and the distress of his profound anxiety:

> It was not really alarming at first, since the change was subtle, but I did notice that my surroundings took on a different tone at certain times: the shadows of nightfall seemed more somber, my mornings were less buoyant, walks in the woods became less zestful, and there was a moment during my working hours in the late afternoon when a kind of panic and anxiety overtook me, just for a few minutes, accompanied by a visceral queasiness – such a seizure was at least slightly alarming, after all. As I set down these recollections, I realize that it should have been plain to me that I was already in the grip of the beginning of a mood disorder, but I was ignorant of such a condition at that time. (Styron 1996, p.59)

Interestingly, despite its prevalence, there are few personal accounts of depression in general textbooks on old age, although Murphy's (1988, p.67) account of some of the experiences of her patients is one exception. Individuals reported:

*   feeling 'a sense of being trapped'
*   thinking 'the future seems hopeless'
*   sensing 'a blank darkness ahead'.

Murphy reminds us of the hardship and suffering behind such feelings: 'Emotions seem empty and shallow... There is often an all-pervading feeling of desolation and irremediable emptiness.'

We need to recognize that, like all forms of mental health disturbance, depression still evokes stigma and prejudice. A survey in 1996 revealed that, in the UK, most people said they would be too embarrassed to go to their GP if they were depressed for fear the GP would think them 'mad' (unbalanced or neurotic) (Priest, Vize and Roberts 1996). For older people this feeling may be more pronounced because of prejudice against and fear of mental illness in the past, and their associations of mental ill-health with asylums and incarceration. Attitudes to depression may be harsh or mistaken, and convey the impression that people should be 'able to snap out of it', or that it is a sign of moral weakness. A recent Age Concern (undated) leaflet on depression tries to counter such beliefs by asserting: 'depression is depression at any age. And nothing to be ashamed of'.

An older person may also be fearful that he or she will be 'put away' or subject to cruel treatment. While these may relate to past views and experiences, more recent portrayals of mental health problems as linked to violence and risk may also influence perceptions of mental health services and people with mental health problems. The 'spoiled identity' (Goffman 1963) of individuals who use mental health services is something that is often neglected when thinking of the impact of a diagnosis of depression upon an older person or upon their family. The impact of this is likely only to be discovered after talking with the person and listening to their concerns. When we suggest 'education' for the person with depression and seek to involve them in treatment decisions, these efforts need to be done in the light of their views about this mental health problem and what it means for them. For some people this may mean that they are suspicious about medication, others may be just as wary of psychological interventions, such as cognitive behavioural therapy, problem solving treatment or interpersonal therapy. As Jorm (2000) states, such general belief systems are important but we know little about how to influence them. This applies particularly to older people.

Some tend to see depression as a sign of weakness of character while others may think of it as a normal part of ageing. Some may seek help from non-medical sources; a recent study of Afro-Caribbean people with depression found they were less likely to seek medical help to mange anxiety and depression than white Europeans. Instead they often went elsewhere, 'This help comprised self-treatment with herbal remedies or seeking support through their local church' (Shaw *et al.* 1999).

Untreated depression impairs quality of life. It also shortens life, not just because of its link to suicide, but because it adds to disability and is linked to physical health problems, for example, heart disease. Older people with depression have higher rates of heart disease than those not depressed. Worse still, often those with heart disease *and* depression do not recover as much or as quickly as individuals who were not depressed. Later life depression is associated with higher than expected rates of illness, disability and even death from a wide range of causes such as brain haemorrhage, pulmonary embolism or bleeding peptic ulcer. This is the aspect of depression that many do not grasp, thinking of it as a psychological disorder in which the only serious risk is from suicide. The opposite is truer. As we described in Chapter 1, depression can be expressed through physical symptoms as much as through changes in mood. It also produces physical symptoms by altering body chemistry, so that thinking and reaction time slow down, clotting mechanisms change and stress hormone levels rise causing high blood pressure, 'furring' of arteries and heart disease.

We need to mention loneliness, which is sometimes confused with depression. There is a strong association with depression symptoms like those given in Chapter 1 and the subjective sense of loneliness, that feeling of being alone and unconnected with others, even when not physically isolated or out of touch with family or friends. Loneliness and depression overlap, but it is possible to be lonely yet not have any depression symptoms at all, and it is therefore wrong to assume that anyone expressing feelings of loneliness is depressed and necessarily suitable for anti-depressant therapy of any kind (Routasalo and Pitkala 2003).

The impact on family and friends

Styron (1996, p.60) recalls the perplexity of his family and friends at what was happening to him at the outset of his depression. As we can see from the range of problems that an older person may experience when depressed, this is a confusing time for relatives who may not know whether the person has an illness or 'is not himself or herself'. This uncertainty is exacerbated if the family is not in frequent contact (see the practice example of Mrs P below).

Practice example: Mrs P, aged 72

Mrs P lives on her own on a housing estate near a seaside town. She moved there with her husband on their retirement and they kept themselves to themselves, with occasional contacts with his family from a first marriage. Mrs P looked after her husband during his terminal illness and his family was grateful for this, and promised to keep in touch. She now often rings her stepson late in the night (she has problems sleeping), with complaints about her loneliness, the noisy neighbours and problems with local teenagers. Her stepson suggests she consider moving, visit her GP, or make some friends but this all seems too difficult for her. He is beginning to resent her demands on his time.

Battison (2004) advises families to listen to their older relative if he or she is reluctant to go to the GP and to discuss their reasons and feelings about why they cannot or think they should not see a doctor. She notes that such arguments 'may be a smokescreen that is hiding a good deal of fear' (p.56). Gradually working towards an agreement that the person will go to see the doctor is a possible aim, and offers to go with them might be appreciated. We discuss the position of carers in a later chapter so here we will look at the wider family and friends, those who are not carers (although may be in the future) or may remain in the circle of family and friends.

While the position of children is now receiving attention in dementia care, so that more thought is being given to explaining the disease and why an older relative is behaving in an apparently strange way (for example, no longer recognizing a grandchild), this subject is not often talked about in respect of depression. Battison (2004) is one of the few who notes that talking to children might be necessary but observes that this can be difficult and painful. She advises that thought is given to telling the child in a way that makes it clear that he or she is not to blame and that telling them is best done early and honestly, and in an age-appropriate way. Similar thought may be needed in respect of how far to tell others in a social circle that an older person has depression. Such is the prevalence of depression that the task may be easier than first realized, and sympathy and understanding more forthcoming than expected.

Withdrawal from social activities may be one of the ways in which an older person tries to cope with the feelings that he or she is experiencing when depressed. A sense of apathy, a sense of having no pleasure, a sense that their aches and pains may be worse if they go outdoors, a fear of falling, all these may contribute to less willingness to retain social contacts and to engage with the sense of reciprocity that underlies relationships with friends, acquaintances and neighbours. Friends, many of whom may be older people themselves, may mistake a person's lethargy for indifference and find that it is difficult to stay involved if the depressed older person does not undertake shared activities, does not return phone calls and is rather preoccupied with his or her own problems. The impact of depression on friends may also reflect fears that it is contagious, and that a group that seeks support for its members and has unwritten rules about 'being cheerful' and 'having a laugh' in adversity may be challenged by those who cannot maintain such a self-image and abide by these codes.

The impact on wider social networks

The impact of depression on wider social networks is not often explored but it may help to explain why attempts to improve social contact and social support seem to be so difficult. We should not be surprised of course that social contact is so hard to refashion or revise, because most of our links with friends and social networks have been built up over many years and through activities such as family contacts, work, shared interests, community involvement and proximity. For many older people these bonds are hard to re-establish, many will have been broken by the death of their peers and may fade with increased social isolation as a result of disability (their own or others'), lack of income and social environments that are often unwelcoming to older people. Relationships with neighbours, for example, are likely to be based on expectations of mutual helpfulness. Neighbours play an important part in providing short-term support (in emergencies for example) but are less likely to provide or be expected to provide long-term support (Bulmer 1987).

It is easy to talk in general terms about the importance of social networks but to forget that they too feel the impact of a person's depression. In the case of Miss V, she may begin to lose contact with the faith group, and her growing isolation may mean that she is not visible in the community, other than being seen as slightly neglectful of her garden and windows. Miss V's fear of young people may mean she starts to shop in places she feels safe, not locally, and that she finds going out or simply 'popping in' to her neighbours is too risky. The neighbourhood has lost someone who provided support to others, felt a sense of community, and participated in social networks. In the language of social capital and civic society, Miss V would be recognized as playing a part in cohesiveness and social well-being. The possibility of depression affects both her and her social circle.

> ### Practice example: Miss V, aged 69
>
> Miss V used to be a 'pillar' of her local faith group, running the girls' group and sorting out the money and bills. The group provided her with great pleasure and she had almost forgotten the tragedies of her earlier life, her collapse into depression and the hospital treatment she endured, but had put behind her. In her late 60s, however, life became more difficult as she felt less able to cope: the financial transactions were getting more complicated and she felt that she was not able to work with the girls in such a friendly way. She found them 'disrespectful', they complained about her audibly. A new pastor appointed a new treasurer, a youth worker took over her role and many of her friends in the congregation were talking about moving away from an area they considered to be in decline. Miss V felt her old anxieties and fears returning.

The impact on practitioners

Biggs (1992) suggests that there is value in thinking about processes of transference and counter-transference in working with older people and that this may provide some way of thinking through some of the difficulties practitioners experience. But few practitioners have the opportunity to reflect on their practice with older people and few training courses explore the impact of depression on those supporting older people. We know that depression may be experienced by those in the caring professions themselves (Manthorpe, Caan and Stanley 2001) and that practitioners often find that their workplace is not sufficiently flexible, understanding or accommodating to their depression. Depressed professionals report, however, that their experiences often give them insight into what it feels like to be depressed and how to use their experiences to support others with similar diagnoses.

The impact of a service user's depression on home carers is less considered, although if a person is dissatisfied, or seems hard to please, or if there is an apparent disparity between what a person can physically do and says he or she can, then a home carer may find this difficult to manage and understand. Twigg (2000) observes that while home care is stressful and its low wages and poor image impact on such workers, the intrinsic rewards of the work derive from the interpersonal relationships between the care worker and service user. The emotional rewards come through the 'warmth of interpersonal exchanges' (Twigg 2000, p.129) and older people's appreciation in part makes up for the work's difficulties. Few home care workers receive much training, many are rushed, and their job is task orientated. This may make it difficult for them to support an older person with depression, and complaints by a service user may further undermine the relationship between worker and home carer.

However, we do know that older people in receipt of home care services are often highly likely to be depressed, with estimates ranging from 24 to 44 per cent of users. A study in the London Borough of Lewisham (Banerjee *et al.* 1996) showed that this was a group with potential to benefit from specific attention from health services. But we consider that home care workers often find themselves carrying the difficulties of work in this area on their own. In contrast to dementia, few training programmes for home care workers focus on depression and its impact on their work and relationships. The importance of making sure that home care workers are as effective as possible is reflected in policy moves that suggest flexible home care is to be given greater priority in service developments (Audit Commission 2000). Judgements by care managers of the potential for mental health services input may not be accurate, and there is an argument for using simple assessment tools to improve detection rates of depression (Préville *et al.* 2004), many of which are illustrated in the Social Care Institute for Excellence Practice Guide (2004).

We outline in Box 2.1 what such a training package might look like, conscious that such training is likely to be brief and could be seen as superficial. But we suggest that depression is so important and the costs of getting support wrong so serious, in terms of wasting opportunities and resources, that it is important to provide care staff with some insight into the impact of depression on service users. Such a model combines the social and medical models of disability and recognizes that home care staff may have important roles in encouraging and practising social contact, in monitoring medication, and in providing the older person with a 'listening ear'.

Box 2.1 Possible outline for information session on depression for home care staff

- What is depression and how might it affect our service users?
- Examples of the problems we face and some ideas for what seems to work well.
- What to do if we think someone is depressed.
- What to do if we think someone is getting worse.
- How to look after ourselves.

Such a training programme and the issues it raises are of similar relevance to staff working in day centres, where there is some evidence that a high percentage of users are depressed but that social contacts are not inevitably improved by attendance (Minardi and Blanchard 2004). In care homes the proportion of services users with depression is generally acknowledged to be high although often unrecognized (Mann *et al.* 2000). The impact on care home staff of a resident's apathy, sleep problems, or agitation can make a stressful job more difficult. We have little evidence, but there are suggestions that people with dementia or depression may be at greater risk than others of elder abuse (Dyer *et al.* 2000).

> ## Practice example: Mrs S, aged 88
>
> Mrs S lives in a care home but is not the most popular among the staff or fellow residents. She refuses to join in social activities and yet complains about being ignored. She is often restless and staff suspect that she rings her bell for attention just when they are 'rushed off their feet'. As one care assistant puts it, 'She thinks she is the only one here we have to look after'. The staff group complains that while other residents are perhaps 'heavier work', 'at least you can laugh with them' and 'some seem to appreciate what you are doing for them' but not Mrs S. Mrs S's depression is recorded in her care plan, but it is not possible to see how this is being responded to. Staff don't really have much idea and think that anything they do will be unlikely to work – so why bother?

The practice example of Mrs S (above), for example, could be repeated in relation to staff on the end of a telephone alarm service who get repeatedly telephoned by an older person with similar anxiety, by voluntary sector schemes who find that they cannot get volunteers to befriend a person who rejects such over-tures, and by emergency services who are rung up by anxious (and, they suspect, simply lonely) older people. We have little evidence of the extent of such problems but they represent ways in which older people with depression are sometimes in contact with a mosaic of services but their depression is so well masked or unrecognized that they are not put in contact with people who can help.

This focus on social care practitioners who are in frequent contact with older people does not mean that social workers are invariably well equipped to undertake advice and co-ordination roles. Many are hesitant and uncertain how the care management process interacts with medical and therapeutic models of assessment and care (Social Care Institute for Excellence 2004). Social workers will increasingly have to undertake standardized measures of assessment of older people (see Chapter 3) as part of the single assessment process rather than referring on to colleagues in the NHS or to specialist social work teams. In turn, their experiences of long-term support of people who are 'hard to engage', their knowledge of social and community networks, and their access to resources to reduce environmental stressors, such as low income, poor housing etc. may be important in providing tailored responses to older people with depression. Older people with alcohol problems (3–4% of older people) may come to the attention of services as a result of increasing failure to cope (perhaps as a result of depression) (Barnes 1997). This group may be very resistant to accepting help, and services too may find that they are not well equipped to meet their needs.

Some work with older people who are homeless suggests that abuse and trauma are common past experiences. Breakdowns in social networks and complex spiralling of problems with accommodation were evident in one recent study (Pannell, Morbey and Means 2002). Depression, while not explicitly identified, may be part of the mental health problems frequently identified as contributory factors to homelessness, causing great reluctance to respond to overtures of support and difficulties in moving back into mainstream accommodation. Its impact on older people with such problems may also be masked by their own perceptions of themselves as 'loners'.

In respect of medicine, Chew-Graham, Baldwin and Burns (2004) suggest that stigma may also explain the relative pessimism surrounding depression among medical practitioners and that GPs may fear opening a 'Pandora's box' if a person appears in the surgery, and thus not explore sufficiently some of the person's feelings or complaints. This may help to explain some of the exasperation reported by family members or other professionals who have worked hard to persuade an older person to get in contact with their GP, only to have the depression seemingly ignored. What can be done in such circumstances? We suggest direct contact with the GP, to clarify your concerns and give detail that the older person may not have divulged.

It is evident that depression also plays a part in people's responses to illness and treatment. For those in hospital following a fall, for example, depression may be an underlying cause of an apparent difficulty in getting back home. Rehabilitation may be more difficult because of a lack of motivation, a sense of apathy or fear of falling again. Being in hospital is likely to lead to changes in mood, and depression is not uncommon among those who have experienced a fall, but the type of depression that lasts and seriously inhibits recovery may respond to treatment and certainly should be investigated. Seeking the advice of an old age psychiatrist may be one way for the nursing staff to explore what is happening to a patient whose behaviour is giving them cause for concern, such as refusing medication or unexplained poor appetite. In some areas there are liaison nurses or medical staff who undertake this role, in others community mental health nurses for older people may come into hospital to support and advise staff. These have developed because the possibility of depression is so often overlooked and also because its existence is not recorded and thus not remembered or addressed by the care or rehabilitation team. Specialist advice may be particularly helpful in distinguishing between problems of depression, dementia and delusion; we discuss these complications further in Chapter 4.

Mulley (2001) provides seven reasons why depression needs to be taken seriously amongst sick older people.

1. They have an increased risk of death from all causes.

2. They have a greater burden of illness and disability.

3. They tend to stay in hospital for longer.

4. They are more likely to move to a care home rather than back home when discharged from hospital.

5. They have reduced levels of both physical and social activity.

6. They have reduced concordance with professional advice (including less co-operation with medical treatments).

7. They are at greater risk of committing suicide.

(Mulley 2001, p.90)

Although this is a very harsh picture of depression, it does capture much of the difficulty that professionals working with depressed older people encounter. Taking depression as a broad category for a moment, we can see that those within it suffer more serious illness for longer, and are harder to treat, often with the least satisfactory outcomes. In practical terms this is important, because we can look at the associations in the opposite way. Those who are hardest to treat, and need longer and more intense input from professionals may also be depressed, and may benefit from their depression being identified, named and addressed. The question is always: how can I best help the person with depression? In the next chapter we focus on interventions that (if more widely employed) can help to reduce the impact of the disabilities and distress that arise from depression.

In summary, the impact of depression ripples out beyond the depressed person and their immediate circle to promote disability, heighten risk, bring about early death and magnify the burden of poor health. These are important points and can be used to argue the case for greater attention to the prevention of depression, more focused training on it and more alert reactions and appropriate responses to older people with depression.

The person with depression may feel 'weak' or even 'mad', and avoid acknowledging his or her problem or engaging with potential sources of help. It is not surprising therefore that depression can put a huge strain on relationships within families, lead to withdrawal from social activities and networks that may be protective or even therapeutic, and undermine the morale, commitment and efforts of professional carers.

CHAPTER 3

Helping Depressed Older People

Helping people with depression can be hard work. For those in health and social care the confidence and capacity to respond to older people with depression may involve a complex mix of factors, not all connected with the illness. Professionals can feel out of their depth with depression, or may find that it resonates with them, bringing back memories of their own distress or that of others close to them. Attitudes to older people can be negative, because they symbolize the loss of abilities that we fear for ourselves, and point out to people focusing on the present that their future is finite and time-limited. Depressed older people can be particularly difficult to encounter and be with, because they transfer powerful emotions, and it can be tempting to avoid the negative feelings they evoke by avoiding the people themselves. Rowe reports that professionals often describe one of two images of their work with people who are depressed: either that they feel as if they are wandering around in a fog, or that they are outside a prison wall and thus unable to reach the person with depression inside (Rowe 2003, p.165). Professionals need a strong framework of understanding to counter these feelings, and one part of that framework is a set of clear roles and responses that can be matched to the situation of each individual. Here we outline some of the elements of that framework.

In our view, the World Psychiatric Association (WPA) is right to describe the general principles of treatment as follows:

1. The most important step is the education of the person (and care givers) about depression, and their involvement in treatment decisions. This means exploring the individual's understanding of their depression, including its causes, and working through any perceptions that may impede efforts to restore normal mood and functioning – depression as 'just desserts', or as a moral fault, for example. It may also mean that the professional has to accept the expertise of the individual, without losing the critical listening faculties that alert others to worsening hopelessness and self-destructive thinking.

2. Doctors, therapists and mental health practitioners treat depression symptoms with the aim of achieving their complete abolition (remission) on the grounds that remaining symptoms are a risk factor for recurrence of depression (Lebowitz, Pearson and Schneider 1997; Judd *et al.* 1998) but do not necessarily aim for 'cure' – not only abolition of symptoms, but also of the chance of relapse. Expectations need to be realistic, both in terms of the speed of recovery (mostly slow) and also the prospects for complete and continuing recovery (which may not happen). A person who may need long-term (even lifelong) anti-depressant treatment needs to have that perspective, and not be left expecting rapid changes or no return of symptoms. Of course, older people who have experienced episodes of depression earlier in life may be very familiar with the relapsing nature of this disorder in them, and may need little convincing that it may not be eradicated from their existence completely. What they may need is the sense that they can enter remission. By its very nature depression erodes optimism, and the life history that might make them (and us) realistic could also breed a sense of hopelessness.

3. Always try to treat the whole person. Other physical disorders, including poor vision and hearing deficits, can make the depressed person more isolated and less capable of helping themselves. For health care staff the message is that they should always signpost the person to appropriate social care agencies and review their medication with a view to withdrawing those unnecessary drug treatments that may alter mood or thinking. For social care workers the message is similar: have all the other possible medical problems been considered, and if present, been dealt with as far as is possible?

4. Monitor the risk of self-harm by first keeping in mind the risk, and also by keeping in contact with the depressed person so that the kinds of sinister changes in mood and behaviour described in Chapter 6 can be recognized and acted upon.

5. Seek medical help or advice from a community mental health nurse for people whom you think have severe depression, using Heywood's (2001) checklist shown in Box 3.1.

(WPA 1999)

Approaches to treatment

There are three main ways to treat depression: with social support, with psychological therapies of various sorts, and with anti-depressant medication. They are not mutually exclusive and there is some evidence that a combination can work better than any one alone. However, all three have passionate advocates and equally strongly motivated enemies. Some older people find it difficult to express their distress in psychological language, while there are others who see anti-depressant medication as dangerous, potentially addictive and a false solution – a sticking plaster – for their problems. Social support and activities may not be what some

---

Box 3.1 Checklist for severe depression

- Are you certain that depression is the right diagnosis?
- Can the right management or therapy be provided?
- Is the outlook for the person better if they stay at home, or do they need hospital care?
- Have their carers the capacity to cope?
- Has the depressed person the capacity to cope?
- Are the home circumstances suitable?
- Have the care staff, nurses or doctors the capacity to cope?

If the answer to any of the above questions is no, then the help of specialist services should be sought (Heywood 2001).

---

depressed older people want, and they will not enjoy them. However, physical activity is increasingly recognized as helpful and cost-effective in the promotion of mental health among older people (Mather *et al.* 2002) and some with depression may find it helpful. Therefore, the kinds of therapies to use need to be negotiated with each person, and this means listening to what the older person wants, thinks and believes. This is why early discussion of explanatory models is so important.

Offering support to depressed older people is associated with quite high rates of recovery (in the sense of freedom from symptoms) (McCusker *et al.* 1998), as anyone who has worked with depressed older people knows, regardless of their actual professional or work role. The home care worker visiting an older person for an hour a week may be an anti-depressant without knowing it, simply by showing an interest in the older person's experience, history and current well-being, relieving anxieties about coping or lifting loneliness.

Offering support to depressed older people is associated with quite high rates of symptomatic recovery (McCusker *et al.* 1998) and reception staff, practice nurses and staff in care homes may have an important therapeutic role (Moxon *et al.* 2001) as important as that of doctors. These kinds of personal relationship may restore a sense of worth that has been eroded by loss of friends and family, long-term illness and loss of abilities or opportunities. Even brief encounters with an empathic and experienced person may help the depressed individual to assimilate losses (developing compensatory mechanisms like new friendships) or to accommodate to them, by changing expectations and standards (Boyd, Mckiernan and Waller 2000). Being able to find or create new social networks and developing meaningful activity seems to promote mental health in later life (Seymour and Gale 2004), although this is not the same as 'solving' the problem of loneliness for those who are already depressed. Volunteering, for example, seems to promote life satisfaction (van Willigen 2000) but many different social activities seem linked to mental and physical well-being (Menec 2003; Warr, Butcher and Robertson 2004). Depression in later life can then be understood to have two possible origins. Individuals may fail to assimilate the challenges to their identity that accompany ageing, and become depressed. Or they may fail to give up past standards that were important to them and become depressed by their failure to retain their former capacity. The conversations that occur within families, among friends or between professionals and service users will reflect these distinctions: what other things can be done to offset social losses or physical disabilities, and what are realistic goals in a changed situation?

We need to acknowledge the power and importance of this everyday approach to depression without romanticizing it, or understating its limitations. Depressed people (of any age) can be demanding and capable of triggering distress in those around them, who may avoid them because they are such hard work. Some people can deal easily with the emotional transference that can occur between the depressed individual and those in contact with them, but others may not be so capable. Similarly, solutions that seem commonsense – befriending the lonely and socially isolated, with the intention of alleviating their depression – may in fact show little evidence of approaches worthy of investment of time and resources (Routasalo and Pitkala 2003). Professional intervention may be a necessary response to worsening depression in an older person, and no more reflects badly (as failure) on those around the depressed individual than it does on the person with the depression. The question for all those working with depressed older people is: what sort of treatment will be best for this individual?

Social support seems to work by altering the thinking and feeling of older people in positive, uplifting ways, but it is not usually consciously psychological; it is simply what people do in productive and reciprocal human relationships. Psychotherapy is different because it is deliberate, framed in terms of psychological theories, frequently conducted on a one-to-one basis outside 'normal' relationships and often intense. Psychological treatments such as those recommended by the *National Service Framework for Older People* (Department of Health 2001) (cognitive behaviour therapy, interpersonal therapy and brief focal analytic psychotherapy) are effective treatments for depressive disorder in older people but are under-used (Lebowitz *et al.* 1997). Age should not be a barrier to referring an older person for psychological therapies (Katona *et al.* 1995), but it often seems to be. A carefully thought out family intervention is associated with an improvement in mood in family carers of people with dementia (Marriott *et al.* 2000). Thus, it falls within the repertoire of social care as much as within the local memory clinic or community mental health trust, but it may be hard to organize. Finally, strengthening self-efficacy by dealing with and overcoming specific problems may be the best way to approach late life depression (Blazer 2002), but as yet there is little evidence from experimental studies to support this, and this is therefore an important area for research.

Medical treatments

Prescribing anti-depressants is a medical task, but everyone should understand the ways in which they can help and should be used, starting with the person concerned and including community nursing staff and the social care workforce. A treatment approach to optimize use of medication in the right doses requires:

1. Choosing a medication with a low risk of adverse effects. This is very important because anti-depressants can cause changes in blood pressure, increase agitation and sleeplessness and (sometimes) alter heart rhythm.

2. A dialogue that elicits specific concerns about medication. The fear that anti-depressants will not alter the underlying disease is in one sense realistic, but most people in pain would not avoid taking pain relief because it does not heal the cause of the pain, so a discussion that acknowledges depression as a symptom worth relieving is sensible. On the other hand, anxiety about becoming dependent on anti-depressants is very reasonable, despite initial assurances that anti-depressants are not habit-forming and given the current concern that it can be difficult to stop taking them.

3. The inclusion of care givers (family members, home care workers, community nurses or care home staff) in educational programmes about depression wherever possible and appropriate (Maidment, Livingstone and Katona 2002).

It is important to know why some treatments are chosen in preference to others, whether you are using them (as a patient or service user), observing their use (as a family member, for example), or providing them (as a doctor or pharmacist). The choice and use of anti-depressant medication should be based on the principles shown in Box 3.2.

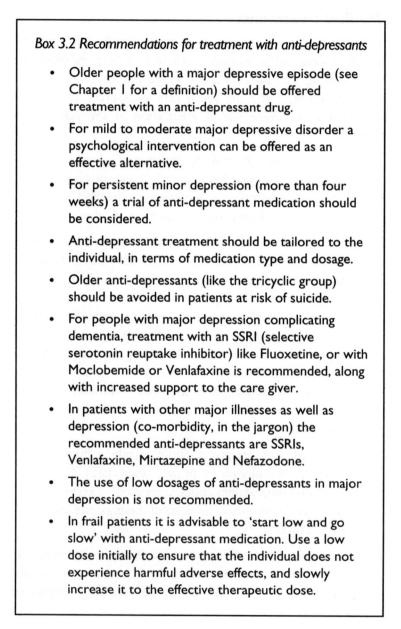

Box 3.2 Recommendations for treatment with anti-depressants

- Older people with a major depressive episode (see Chapter 1 for a definition) should be offered treatment with an anti-depressant drug.

- For mild to moderate major depressive disorder a psychological intervention can be offered as an effective alternative.

- For persistent minor depression (more than four weeks) a trial of anti-depressant medication should be considered.

- Anti-depressant treatment should be tailored to the individual, in terms of medication type and dosage.

- Older anti-depressants (like the tricyclic group) should be avoided in patients at risk of suicide.

- For people with major depression complicating dementia, treatment with an SSRI (selective serotonin reuptake inhibitor) like Fluoxetine, or with Moclobemide or Venlafaxine is recommended, along with increased support to the care giver.

- In patients with other major illnesses as well as depression (co-morbidity, in the jargon) the recommended anti-depressants are SSRIs, Venlafaxine, Mirtazepine and Nefazodone.

- The use of low dosages of anti-depressants in major depression is not recommended.

- In frail patients it is advisable to 'start low and go slow' with anti-depressant medication. Use a low dose initially to ensure that the individual does not experience harmful adverse effects, and slowly increase it to the effective therapeutic dose.

How should treatments be tailored to individuals? To some extent this depends on their personal history, other medical problems and their preferences, but the nature and depth of the depression also matters. An approach to deciding on treatment options for the different types of depressive disorder has been developed by the Royal College of Psychiatrists' Faculty of Old Age Psychiatry (Royal College of Psychiatrists 2002), and is shown in Table 3.1.

Table 3.1 Type of depression and treatment modality

Type of depression	*Treatment modality*
Psychotic depression	Combined anti-depressant or ECT – urgent referral indicated
Severe/major (non-psychotic) depression	Combined anti-depressant and psychological therapy – consider referral
Mild – moderate depressive episode	Anti-depressant *or* psychological therapy (CBT, problem solving, IPT or brief psychodynamic psychotherapy)
Dysthymia	Anti-depressant
Recent onset sub-threshold (minor) depression	Watchful waiting and support
Persistent sub-threshold (minor) depression	Anti-depressant and support
Brief depression, grief reaction and bereavement symptoms	Treat as for moderate depression if duration and intensity suggest intervention is indicated; otherwise support and watchful waiting
Persistent minor depression with co-morbidity	Some evidence of the effectiveness of counselling

Source: Royal College of Psychiatrists 2002

It is a rough rule of thumb, and may be contested by those who do not start from a medical perspective and who would give greater weight to psychological approaches than to medication. We offer it here because it does offer a menu of options that will be used when older people with depression encounter medical care.

Tailoring can be a matter of informed judgement rather than a strict science for there is no evidence that one anti-depressant is more effective than another. The choice of medication will be determined by patient characteristics such as:

- severity of depression – favouring tricyclics

- safety – favouring newer anti-depressants

- prior response to a particular medication

- tolerability – are there side effects, and if so are they so unpleasant that it is better not taking the treatment?

- anticipated side effects

- drug interactions

- concordance – to what extent does the individual understand the problem, accommodate to the diagnosis and its treatment, and assimilate the therapy into everyday routines?

- frailty

- local protocols – the rules and guidelines on medication use produced by primary care trusts (PCTs).

Newer anti-depressants like the SSRIs are better tolerated than older drugs (like the tricyclics) but the difference is not great (Anderson, Nutt and Deakin 2000).

What should be done when treatment seems to fail in those instances when anti-depressants do not change the mood or energy of the depressed person, and psychological approaches are either not accepted at all or do not appear to have an effect? Some old age psychiatrists will suggest electro-convulsive therapy

(ECT), a controversial treatment that involves triggering a convulsion by giving a powerful electric shock to the brain of the anaesthetized patient. There is an argument that ECT is more effective in older people than in younger people with depression, but at the price of worsening memory loss (Katona 1994). Over half of those who receive ECT in the UK are aged over 65 years of age (Leason 2004) (over 1000 people each year) but the National Institute of Clinical Excellence (2003) has recommended that this treatment is restricted until more is known about its effects on memory, quality of life and general health. This advice is not universally accepted, with some US researchers arguing that ECT improves both quality of life and health (McCall, Dunn and Rosenquist 2004).

Long-term treatment

How long should anti-depressant treatments continue? The best evidence on continuation and maintenance treatment regimes, as summarized by the Royal College of Psychiatrists (2002), suggests that:

- maintenance therapy of 12 months for a first major depressive episode and longer for a recurrent disorder, would be appropriate, but also that there is less certainty about treatment for non-major depression

- Nortriptyline, Dosulepin (Dothiepin), Citalopram and Paroxetine can prevent recurrence

- there is a lack of consensus on how long maintenance treatment should last, whether indeed it should last for life.

These guidelines are imprecise, and decisions need to be made on a person-by-person basis. The scientific evidence also changes; for example, Paroxetine is no longer an anti-depressant that would be offered to older people, because of the risks of dependency and adverse effects.

Read the practice example below, and work out the strategy that you would use to try and help this person.

Practice example: Mrs T, aged 90

Mrs T has lived alone since her husband died 30 years ago, but she has friends who speak with her every day by phone, and visitors once or twice a week. She employs a cleaner to help in the house for an hour every week, but is proud that she can keep her home in the orderly fashion that she likes. Five months ago her cat was killed on the busy road outside her home, and she has not been sleeping well since, often waking in the night and finding it difficult to return to sleep. Although scornful of 'doctor-botherers' and an infrequent attender at her local surgery she visits her GP asking for sleeping tablets. She looks depressed, admits to her doctor that life is not worth living and agrees to take Dothiepin (one of the older generation of anti-depressants) in the dose of 75mg at night. After a month she is sleeping better but remains depressed with a poor appetite. A week later her neighbour requests a home visit because Mrs T has fallen after feeling dizzy. Her GP changes her medication to Fluoxetine 20mg a day, but a month later she is once again complaining of sleeplessness. A telephone discussion between the GP and the local old age psychiatrist results in a referral for specialist assessment, but only after a number of tests have been done to check that she does not have an under-active thyroid gland, irregular heart rhythm or low blood pressure.

Learning points

Mrs T is probably relatively robust, both psychologically and physically, but her coping strategies are upset by an adverse event – the death of her cat – resulting in a depressive illness.

The doctor's response – to give her an anti-depressant – is understandable, given her tendency not to complain, the seriousness of insomnia as a symptom and the duration of her depression. What we do not know from this story is to what extent her social network was helping her with her loss, and therefore we cannot gauge how useful extra social support, or some focussed counselling, could be.

Medication adverse effects and dosages matter, and side effects can make the person's situation worse, so careful prescribing is important. The first anti-depressant prescribed may have a sedative effect, so helping Mrs T to sleep, but the dose may not have been sufficient to lift her depressed mood, and the duration of use too short to be certain about its lack of benefit. Changing to a new generation anti-depressant has advantages: fewer side effects overall, and disadvantages: stimulant effects may restore a symptom like insomnia.

The investigations for thyroid gland failure, cardiac rhythm abnormalities and falling blood pressure are important because the first can produce depression symptoms while the latter two may produce apparent drug adverse effects.

What therapies should the old age psychiatrist suggest? The best known is cognitive behavioural therapy (CBT), a time-limited therapy, often taking up to six sessions that address and counteract negative ways of thinking. 'It offers a framework for assessing the pattern of behaviour in service users and a method for altering their thinking, feeling and behaviour' (Walker and Beckett 2003, p.27). Through this framework people can be helped to become more self-aware, to make connections between their ideas and their feelings, and to develop or re-learn ways of coping with difficult or intruding thoughts. CBT can be delivered by psychiatrists or mental health practitioners and should be part of the repertoire of available responses for older people, especially those living in care homes. It has been found effective but a major review of talking therapies did not find many studies of older people receiving such support (Gloaguen *et al.* 1998), although Burkhardt (1987) reports that improvements in mental health are evident in older people receiving any kind of therapy. Interpersonal therapy can be complex and is primarily carried out by psychologists, currently in short supply in work with older people. Brief psychological treatments do not always include older people (Churchill *et al.* 2001) and again their availability is limited. Nevertheless, primary care trusts and partnership boards that commission services for older people should be able to identify local services. If these are not available, those with an interest in older people's mental health ought be arguing that they need to be developed. As we shall discuss further in Chapter 9, great variations in the quantity and quality of therapeutic services for older people restrict our abilities to help to an extent that is no longer tolerated for other age groups.

CHAPTER 4

Depression and Dementia

Depression and dementia can be hard to tell apart, because they so often occur together. As Cheston and Bender (1999) note, one of the most common referrals that is presented to mental health practitioners in health and social services concerns an older person who 'seems to be withdrawn, forgetful and tearful or in low spirits' (p.153). Depression and dementia can occur in the same person at the same time, and each can mimic the other. Depressed older people may notice that their memory is not working as well or as fast as it did before, and be more concerned about that change – which they fear is due to Alzheimer's disease – than about the loss of concentration, sleeplessness and mood changes that accompany it. In the early stages of dementia individuals who notice that they cannot think as they did before may become depressed about their loss of ability, but their memory loss will be different. In depression memory is slowed, but the name or date being searched for is eventually remembered, whilst in dementia it may not return at all, especially if it concerns recent events. We have all experienced this, in situations where we meet an acquaintance but cannot recall their name, or find ourselves standing in a room thinking 'Why did I come in here?' It happens when we are tired, as every parent of small children knows, and it happens when we are preoccupied, but not to the extent that it does with a depressive illness. The name does come back to us, and we do remember what we were looking for, even if the cause of this memory loss is depression. People with early dementia write lists, put notices on doors as reminders, get telephoned by friends or family members to prompt them to do things, or otherwise organize their external world to replace the lost short-term memory, before they are diagnosed.

Apathy can be a feature of dementia that is mistaken for depression, but is subtly different from the inability to enjoy oneself found in depression. The apathetic individual will often respond to activity initiated by another and enjoy it, while in depression a person's mood may improve during the course of the day, but not necessarily in response to personal contact (Weiner 2004). Sleep disturbance may be profound in depression, with individuals waking in the early hours and not being able to return to sleep, while depression promotes lowering of self-esteem in a way that dementia does not.

Other features of changed behaviour that point to depression rather than dementia are:

- a relatively short period of time between the onset of the change, and a consultation with a doctor or other professional

- a previous history of depression or anxiety

- more certainty about exactly when the changes began

- a tendency to give 'I don't know' answers

- impairment of recent and distant memory, equally.

(Harris 2004)

One of the problems with much home care provision is that different staff, some of whom may only meet once or infrequently, support older people such as Mr E. Home care workers often have hectic schedules and lack time to build up relationships or to get to know the people they are supporting. How can a changing series of different and busy home care workers realize that Mr E is not his usual self? How can they know if he is any better or worse

Practice example: Mr E, aged 86

Mr E lives alone, supported by home care workers because of his blindness. He complains that his memory is getting worse, and that he cannot remember people's names or where he has put things. He has become less talkative over the last few weeks, changing from cheerful and interested in each new carer and their lives to being unforthcoming and concerned only with practical things in his everyday life.

Learning points

Does he have early signs of dementia or is he becoming depressed? It may often be difficult to know; what may be important is that a home carer may be able to suggest that a check up by the doctor could be helpful, perhaps offering to go with Mr E or to arrange the appointment, or transport, or a home visit. The GP may find the home carer can also help as an advisor, in the absence of family members.

Her observations about Mr E's behaviour will assist the GP, as withdrawal can be a feature of depression and those who complain about memory loss usually do not have dementia.

Nonetheless, as up to 40 per cent of those with early dementia have been found in some studies to have depression symptoms, dementia may be present and the care plan for Mr E will need to be adapted to reflect this possibility, such as making sure that he has greater continuity of workers and that his medication can be managed. Person centred planning, as a system in social care services, may have much to offer here, although it is mainly used in relation to people with learning disabilities.

at remembering names, and who can they talk to about their concerns? On a personal level, how can an individual care worker get over the feeling that she is being rather judgemental if she comments on Mr E, and will these be seen as relevant to the home care contract anyway?

We cannot answer these questions, but use them to illustrate the importance of monitoring care services and to point to the difficulties of providing sensitive support for people such as Mr E whose needs may be seen as low level and 'merely' practical. Care workers with limited time, often little training and a series of tasks to complete in a hurry, are not often valued as the listening ears of social and health care services, especially in regard to mental health problems. But for people such as Mr E, with no family near, they are key to picking up small changes, if their service encourages such communication. When policy talks about the importance of integrated care and whole systems, it is the circumstances of people like Mr E it should be considering as well as the work of professionals and the world of budgets and plans.

Dementia and its diagnosis

The diagnosis of dementia and the breaking of the bad news itself may trigger depression, as the reality of present losses and the prospect of further loss appear while the individual affected can still think about their implications. One UK study estimates that 63 per cent of people with Alzheimer's disease also suffer from depression symptoms (Burns, Jacoby and Levy 1990). Another from the US reports that 30 per cent of people with Alzheimer's disease met the criteria for major depression (Teri and Reifler 1997). A collapse of assumptions can become evident as a person begins to realize that his or her memory is failing, that his or her body and brain are no longer functioning properly, and that everything in life is now uncertain and potentially unstable (Bender 2003). Feelings such as turmoil, helplessness, and diminished self-esteem are evident when people with newly recognized early dementia talk together in support groups (Snyder *et al.* 1995). The reluctance of many professionals to disclose the diagnosis is understandable, given this risk, for many do not know how they will be able to help the person who finds such news so difficult that a depression develops. Many are also fearful of making an incorrect diagnosis by labelling a person who has depression as having dementia (Gove 2002, p.29). When members of the family ask that the diagnosis be withheld from a person with dementia, they may be trying to avoid the collapse of coping strategies that can occur with the breaking of bad news. The question for general practitioners, nurses or social workers is how should this diagnosis be shared with the person with dementia (and their family), when should this be done, and by whom? The answers to these questions will be determined in part by the experience of the professionals – those with expertise in dealing with disability are likely to be best equipped – and in part by the support mechanisms in place for the person concerned, and those around them.

Clearly, many of the discussions that practitioners might have with a person who has early dementia – about their future wishes, fulfilling some of their ambitions and dreams or making plans for living arrangements and finances – may be matters that might prove difficult for a person with depression. Such a person may not feel up to attending some of the support groups that provide self-help or others with therapeutic aims. Many such groups provide a valuable social function, as the group described by Cheston and Jones (2002) makes apparent. This sense of sociability may be worrying for a person with depression. If this is so, practitioners may like to consider:

- offering to join and stay with a person during the group

- encouraging relatives or carers to make use of support groups even if the person they are supporting does not want to attend, or attend at this time

- setting up one-to-one professional or volunteer visits at home, equipped with an outline of the support group's programme to provide the person with the same information to some degree

- asking another member of the group to make contact with the person before a meeting so as to reduce the worry of not knowing anyone
- talking to group leaders about their possible difficulties and ways of accommodating a person with depression in some or all of the group's activities.

Breaking bad news

Is there a way to prevent depression developing as a result of breaking the news about dementia? We can answer this question by saying that there is no established way of preventing depression but that we are accumulating evidence from people with dementia about what they found more or less supportive in hearing their diagnosis. Elements relevant to depression include:

- taking time to explain the diagnosis
- making follow up appointments, and using these to ask about the person's feelings and mood
- providing some written information
- not emphasizing what will happen at later stages
- having time to respond to questions
- letting people know of local support and offering to provide an introduction.

It is, of course, likely to be a medical practitioner who will break the news, but many professionals report that they continue to answer people's queries about dementia and 'go over' the information that people have been given in medical contexts. All need to be aware of the risk of depression and how to minimize this as well as knowing how to support people if it should develop.

Depression in dementia's middle and later stages

Many personal testimonies reflect the difficulties of acquiring support for a person with depression who has a diagnosis of dementia. Nurock (2002), for example, provides an account of the ways in which professionals appeared more ready to consider that she might be depressed as a carer rather than the possibility that her husband might have depression:

> I knew my husband was depressed too. He was very aware of his deteriorating mental faculties. It was suggested that I try him on my pills – but they only made his confusion worse. What about psychotherapy? 'Wouldn't help', I was told, 'He would forget what was being said!' Undaunted, I found a suitable psychologist – privately of course – whom Leonard saw regularly for nearly a year. It helped enormously. He always left there looking happier and more at peace with the world: that alone was worthwhile even if the effect didn't last. (Nurock 2002, p.67)

Some of the resistance to identifying, let alone treating depression in people with dementia comes from a negative perception of dementia itself, but there is also a realistic anxiety about giving medication which affects the brain to someone whose brain is no longer working as it did. Uncertainties about the possible interaction between the new 'anti-dementia drugs' (ACEI inhibitors) and anti-depressants, or the risks of a depressive response to stopping ACEI inhibitors, are also likely to cause anxiety in doctors. What is more disconcerting is the widespread belief that psychological approaches have no role in treating depression in people with dementia.

We suggest a series of points for practitioners to consider when supporting someone whose disabilities arising from their dementia are worsening. The aim is to lessen the likelihood that the person will become depressed by:

- supporting the person to achieve as much as they can but avoiding, as far as possible, feelings of failure

- trying to make the most of the person's sense of humour
- providing stimulating but not too confusing environments
- keeping time for personal contact that provides comfort, touch and emotional warmth (e.g. hand massage, hair brushing)
- being aware if reminiscence or reality orientation is becoming stressful
- helping relatives to 'be there' and not to feel they need to make sure the person is firmly in the present.

Hospital care

As with dementia itself, the possibility of a person having both dementia and depression may become evident in hospital. This is where an older person who may have been 'managing' fairly well in an isolated way at home falls under the professional spotlight. Following an operation or an infection, an older person may seem to have problems with memory, may be thought to be hallucinating and may be very upset. If this is a temporary delirium it may be cleared up by treatment such as antibiotics or decrease after a short time. However, it may expose the older person to scrutiny about exactly how he or she is managing or whether he or she will respond to rehabilitation and be able to return home.

For hospital staff, the impact of depression among older patients (as discussed in Chapter 2) can be that recovery is slower. If depression is accompanied by a dementia the impact of this may be perplexing, with the older person understandably upset at times and relatives also anxious and confused. We suggest that the following network of support may be helpful to practitioners, such as nurses, helping a patient with depression and dementia who is in hospital for a physical health problem, such as a broken leg or following a hip replacement:

1. liaison with mental health professionals, nurses or psychiatrists who can help facilitate communication between services and help to ensure that mental health assessment continues after a hospital stay

2. systems whereby local mental health community nurses make regular visits to wards, talk to the nurses and other staff, help with assessments and provide a bridge to the care home or home, again providing continuity

3. intermediate care teams that contain specialists in rehabilitation of people who have mental health problems, who can work directly with the person but also with the staff who will be continuing the rehabilitation.

Returning home, any care package, whether this is part of a social services care management system or a case management approach led by the primary care team, needs to take on board the potential needs caused by the interaction of dementia and depression. We suggest the following points should inform the single assessment process; many of them would apply to anyone but the emphasis on certain points may be heavier.

1. How has the person been supported since they learned that they had dementia?

2. What do we know about the person's coping skills and how these have been working since they learned of the diagnosis of dementia?

3. Has the person had anything like depression in the past, perhaps a bad attack of the 'baby blues', a great deal of 'trouble with nerves' and what do they feel helped?

4. What does the person think about the role and value of medication and its impact, both in respect of dementia and depression (together with any other items they may be using for either, and for any other complaints)?

5. What are the person's likes and dislikes (former as well as current) and what might they wish for the future?

6. What are carers and family members finding difficult, what have they been told and who is supporting them?

7. What is recorded in care plans or the assessment of need documentation (such as those for the single assessment process)? Who is this information shared with?

Whatever their roles and settings, practitioners need a 'high index of suspicion' of depression among older people (Hughes 1999), and this applies to those who may be classed as having dementia, as much as anything else. Service alignments that divide older people into groups, according to whether they have an organic or functional mental health problem, or into dementia services and the rest, run the risk of creating compartments that focus on one condition to the exclusion of the possibility of any other. As Cheston and Bender note (1999) the 'two clinical diagnoses tend to be seen as two separate entities'. They continue:

> In many ways separating out the apparent decline in the person's cognitive functioning caused by dementia from any changes in their emotional state arising from non-organic causes is an impossible feat: it is perfectly possible for the two to co-exist. (p.153)

A wide range of negative events can have a profound impact on people with dementia, triggering a depressive episode. This may be another illness, an injury, the loss of someone important or a traumatic incident, like a burglary. The role of victim support schemes can be particularly helpful in helping to restore an older person's sense of control and to lessen their feelings of self-blame. As with many things, it may not be the scale of the loss itself that prompts the depression but the signal that this gives to the older person that things seem out of control and that they live in an apparently hostile world.

Practice example: Mr W, aged 78

Mr W had worked into his 70s, and retired reluctantly. He spent his time after retirement pottering about, but as the years passed did less and less, largely giving up gardening and cooking, both of which had been passions, instead sitting and looking out over his garden, now tended by his wife. He was quiet, but mostly agreeable if a bit vague with others, only getting irritated by his loud and boisterous grandchildren. His mood changed abruptly when his son-in-law died suddenly, and he spent hours each day crying, in response to any mention of the dead man, but also in reaction to sad events reported on the television news. It was this seeming change in his personality that prompted Mrs W to ask the doctor what was happening to her husband.

Depression can also superimpose itself on dementia in the later stages of the disease process, sometimes appearing as changes in behaviour in an individual who is seemingly well supported at home or in a care home. As with early separation of depression and dementia, the task of working out why behaviour has changed may be difficult. One rule of thumb that we think is useful is the mnemonic 'PAID' (originating from the Institute of Psychiatry), which asks whether the behaviour change is attributable to:

- Physical problems, like a bladder infection or painful arthritis, where treatment with antibiotics or pain-killers may alter behaviour.

- The activities of others, which the person finds distressing. This may be being washed or bathed, or receiving other types of intimate care, but it may be something less obvious that has profound significance for the individual.

- Intrinsic features of dementia, like 'wandering' or stroking items of clothing, which are either inconvenient for or misunderstood by carers.

- Depression (or delusions). Depression may induce agitation in the affected person, and delusions (for example, property being stolen) are relatively common in dementia.

In other circumstances the care in a home may be less than adequate for the whole person, confining itself to the admittedly important tasks of keeping the body clean, warm and comfortable. As Marshall (2001) observes, there are very low expectations for people with dementia in care homes:

> Many staff may still believe that people with dementia are unaware of the world and unable to benefit from interaction. The inevitability of decline, which is so often emphasised in definitions of dementia, does not encourage staff to see their interactions as therapeutic… It is all too easy to blame the dementia for the extent to which patients spend their time sleeping or sitting apathetically around the walls of the communal areas. In a sense dementia lets staff at all levels and those responsible for the quality of care, off the hook. (pp.410–411)

As we outline in Chapter 7, the experience of caring for someone with dementia can itself produce a depressive disorder. In people with dementia a structured family intervention has been associated with an improvement in mood in care givers (Marriott *et al.* 2000) and this may work too with people who are supporting someone with depression and dementia, and the complexities of such symptoms. Promising evidence from involving families and people with dementia in enjoyable activities together suggests that this may help reduce depression in both the family member and the person with dementia (Teri and Logsdon 1991). Teri *et al.*'s later (1997) study of people with dementia who were depressed and their carers suggests that if they receive help

---

Practice example: Mrs M, aged 84

Maureen, the home care assistant with responsibility for Mrs M's care, had got to know Mr M very well. He visited his wife daily and prompted her to make the most of her memory and skills, sometimes insistently. Maureen began to notice that after her husband's visits Mrs M kept referring to herself as 'stupid, stupid'. Maureen found the opportunity to talk about this with her colleagues over lunch one day and, as a result, plucked up courage to talk to Mr M about perhaps letting his wife respond to him at her own pace. Mrs M then began to be less upset, even though her dementia was steadily worsening.

---

with problem solving and with getting involved in pleasurable activities, as compared with receiving standard care, then the depression of both groups is reduced.

Treatments

Depression associated with early dementia can be disabling in its own right, and is worth treating with medication and psychosocial support. On balance, the best anti-depressant medication is the selective serotonin reuptake inhibitor (SSRI) group of drugs, like Fluoxetine (Prozac), but there have been doubts about some members of this group of medicines because of serious adverse effects and at least one – Paroxetine (Seroxat) – should not be used by older people.

In the later stages of dementia the symptoms of depression, like sleep disturbance or profound loss of appetite, can be treated if they are causing significant distress to the individual, but this is a task for a specialist. Timely discussion with an old age psychiatrist or a community mental health nurse should be the first step in relieving distress. It is likely that they will be able to make a treatment plan and they will have an important role in talking to family members or support staff to let them know how to accommodate the behaviour of the depressed person and implement the treatment plan. One important part of their role is to let carers know how and when this level of service should be contacted, giving such details in advance and, of course, making sure that the information covers times such as nights and weekends.

Policy

Dementia is less common in later life than depression, but has a higher profile. There are national Alzheimer's societies around the world, but no depression societies – depression fits under a broader label, as in the Mental Health Foundation, or is part of a broader agenda, as with Age Concern. Dementia has the *Journal of Dementia Care* that acts as a trade journal for all those concerned with dementia care, but there is no similar publication for those working with depressed older people. And while depressed people may be told to 'pull themselves together', who would say to a person with dementia 'just remember!'

CHAPTER 5

Depression, Anxiety and Psychosis

Anxiety may be the most visible feature of depression in later life, but not every older person who is anxious is also depressed. The way we might respond to anxiety and depression is likely to be different, so how can we distinguish between anxiety as a symptom of depression, and anxiety as a symptom in its own right?

We all use our past experience to understand other people's behaviour, and fit new encounters into our personal theories that we have built up over time, using the knowledge that we have gained from practical activity as well as from study. We all recognize patterns, and when called on to do so we all try to solve problems, whether we are home care workers, community nurses or old age psychiatrists, but the patterns we recognize and the solutions we seek are different. Part of these differences stems from the different training of different groups of people working with older people, and part from the exposure that different disciplines have to depression. Those who work almost exclusively with depressed older people, like old age psychiatrists, will develop complex images of how depression shows itself in people with very different personalities, and how it affects others. Those who work with a wider range of people and problems – say, pharmacists – may have a less complex set of ideas about depression, and be less likely to spot its early signs or its subtle expressions.

This matters because access to services, and therefore to treatments for depression, may depend on people whose judgements and observational skills may be less powerful than are needed if depression is to be correctly identified, named (diagnosed) and treated. The pharmacist may notice that a regular older customer buys a lot of medicines, vitamins or tonics over the counter, but see this as perhaps the mild end of hypochondriasis. General practitioners faced with the complexity of late life mental health disorders will tend to use pattern recognition and problem solving logic in an attempt to assist their patients. If the patterns learned by the general practitioner, either formally through education or informally through experience, are less complex than the reality some other problem will be 'recognized': anxiety, insomnia or physical symptoms. Action will then be taken to solve these perceived problems, even if the medication prescribed – typically a pain-killer or a sleeping tablet – may not be appropriate for depression.

So once again all those who work with older people are in a difficult position of not knowing how to interpret their complaints, concerns and behaviours with any certainty. Anxiety may be obvious, but is there such a thing as uncomplicated anxiety in later life, or is all anxiety expressed by older people a sign of depression, until proved otherwise? Our impression from both social care and clinical experience, and from reviewing the literature, is that anxiety does exist as an entity independently of depression, which can be recognized not so much through its specific content of expressed worries and fears (Diefenbach, Stanley and Beck 2001), as by the presence of physical, cognitive and/or behavioural symptoms and signs of anxiety, as shown in Box 5.1.

The important question is whether the anxious older person also has the depression symptoms given in Chapter 1. If they do, it matters because their depression should be treated as a priority and not 'missed' because the anxiety symptoms are so dominant. If they do not have features of depression, paying attention to the anxiety symptoms alone is logical. The symptoms of combined depression and anxiety may be reduced, and quality of life

---

Box 5.1 Common symptoms of anxiety

Physical

Palpitations, dry mouth, urinary frequency, dizziness, 'pins and needles' feelings, difficulty in breathing and hyperventilation, nausea, tremor, chest tightness, pallor, sweating and cold skin.

Cognitive

Nervousness, feelings of dread, distractibility, inability to relax, apprehension, panic, insomnia and irritability.

Behavioural

Hyperactivity, pressured speech, seeking reassurance, repetitive activity, phobias and being very easily startled.

---

improved, by use of selective serotonin reuptake inhibitors (SSRIs) like Fluoxetine ('Prozac') (Doraiswamy 2001). However, older individuals with a mixture of anxiety and depression symptoms have more severe physical illnesses (Lenze, Mulsant *et al.* 2001), seem more likely to discontinue anti-depressant medication, are less likely to respond if they continue and are likely to have shorter remissions even when treatment works (Flint and Rifat 1997), than depressed older patients without anxiety symptoms.

In situations where anxiety symptoms exist but there is no underlying depression, treatment options are bounded by the hazards of medication on one hand and the uncertain acceptability or effectiveness of psychological treatments on the other. Doctors prescribe, but medication for anxiety in later life is even more problematic than in younger people. The most commonly prescribed anxiety-reducing medications used by older people in the UK are the benzodiazepine group, which includes Temazepam, Diazepam ('Valium') and Nitrazepam ('Mogadon'). Another group, the 'Z' drugs (Zopiclone, Zolpiderm), is also becoming popular.

These medicines can produce problems of physical slowing and sedation, especially with widely used long-acting preparations like Diazepam and Nitrazepam (Kirby, Denihan *et al.* 1999). Benzodiazepines are poorly handled by the body's metabolism, and accumulation of them in the blood and brain is associated with falls, confusion and inhibition of the brain's breathing regulator, which is potentially disastrous for an older person with, say, severe bronchitis. Unsupported, sudden withdrawal from benzodiazepines may precipitate 'rebound' anxiety or confusion. As treatments for anxiety symptoms they are only useful in short-term course; psychological approaches are preferable as longer term approaches to anxiety in older people.

Psychological treatments for anxiety, including relaxation, cognitive behavioural therapy, psychodynamic therapy and life review, are possible alternatives to medication use (Wetherell 1998). Psychological approaches to treatment of anxiety symptoms may seem to offer more appropriate first line therapy than current medication, but their effectiveness is unclear, and a widespread, if inaccurate, view that older people have little insight and are unable to deal with their problems in psychological terms may limit the options made available. The techniques that can be deployed include relaxation methods, cognitive behavioural approaches like guided imagery, systematic desensitization and re-attribution, and family therapies (McWilliam, Stewart and Brown 1999). While the evidence base for these methods is slight, they may offer some scope for intervention with the phobic older person seeking (and getting) increased but inappropriate support at home from family, neighbours and community services. Fear of street crime, for example, is common in the older generation, but there is no reason to believe that a chronic state of fear, with disabling generalized avoidance behaviour that is dismissed euphemistically as 'nervousness' or 'loss of confidence', is a normal or inevitable consequence of growing old (Lindesay 1997). The strong association of anxiety and hypochondriacal concerns (excessive worries about health or illness that are unfounded) may be important for primary care practitioners to review in relation to older people who visit their general practitioners frequently (Bravo and Silverman 2001). The tendency to recognize those with the most severe symptoms, but to miss those with less severe symptoms, is replicated in the provision of therapies. Psychosocial treatments are offered to those with the highest levels of anxiety and depression. However, people with physical illnesses and pain who do not offer or accept psychological explanations of their symptoms receive fewer psychosocial interventions and outcomes for them are worse (Fritsche, Sandholzer and Werner 2000).

High levels of anxiety and depression may be evident in response to certain events, such as waiting for tests. Cheston and Bender (1999) report that people waiting for assessment in respect of their memory may be greatly at risk of anxiety and depression and that the process of the tests can create yet more anxiety and tension (p.198). They suggest that a spiral of anxiety and depression may be formed, and that those professionals who are involved in such testing and assessments need to be keenly aware of the emotional and social contexts of their work. This means that:

- people should be told what is going on
- their specific worries should be addressed
- their risk of depression should be considered and discussed.

Among older people with Alzheimer's disease anxiety and depression can exist together, with one US study (Teri *et al.* 1999) showing that 70 per cent of older people with Alzheimer's disease living at home showed anxiety symptoms and 54 per cent had both anxiety and depression symptoms. Within this group, difficulties with activities of daily living and challenging behaviours were common. Such figures suggest the benefit of practitioners asking about such problems and helping carers by providing them with information and services or support that can reduce their difficulties. They also suggest the value of thinking not about people as

Practice example: Mr G, aged 79

Mr G is seen at home by his GP. His home care worker, Mrs K, reports that he is very anxious and always seeking reassurance that his health is not deteriorating, and that he will continue to receive care. His wife died two years ago, and nine months ago he had a stroke that left him confined to a wheelchair. He denies being depressed but admits to not enjoying anything, saying, 'How would you feel in my position?' He has difficulty sleeping, has lost weight and refuses Meals on Wheels because 'they taste awful'. One month ago he started to experience urinary incontinence but says it is 'just part of getting old' and that nothing can be done. Mrs K vainly tries to get him to see his doctor and reports back to her supervisor that the work is getting beyond her.

Learning points

Anxiety can mask depression, and in his case Mr G has two triggers for depression: his wife's death and his disability following the stroke.

His physical changes suggest either that he is developing a severe depressive illness or has a new, as yet unrecognized, disease process, so both of these possibilities need investigating further.

Anhedonia – loss of pleasure – is more common as a dominant symptom in late life depression than guilt.

Mr G needs his care package reviewed, particularly as he might be at risk of losing someone who knows him well. This needs to be done in conjunction with professionals from the stroke service, his health care team, and with the involvement of Mrs K. The single assessment process needs to look at both his physical and mental health needs.

being either depressed or having dementia but that many are likely to have a complex combination of depression, anxiety and dementia. In a case study discussed by James and Sabin (2002), for example, a person with Parkinson's disease and related dementia had a history of anxiety and of social phobias. It took time to gain his trust so as to make a proper assessment of his dementia, as the man adopted a range of safety seeking behaviours that meant he avoided contact and gave the impression that his memory was worse than it was. Reducing his anxiety by cognitive behavioural approaches helped lessen his anxiety and increased his contact with fellow care home residents.

Psychosis

Psychotic disorders in old age are overshadowed by dementia and depression, both of which occur more commonly, but they are no less problematic for the primary care doctor or nurse to diagnose or manage, or for social care staff to support, and very difficult for family and social networks. In older people the main feature of psychosis is the delusion that the individual is being persecuted in some way, although up to 60 per cent of individuals with this symptom will also have depression symptoms, and a minority will have some form of dementia (Howard 2001). Among the delusions there can be powerful beliefs about physical symptoms and illnesses, and 'partition' beliefs – in which walls or doors do not stop people passing through them.

The research literature about psychoses affecting older people that could guide practitioners is sparse, compared with that for the commoner psychiatric disorders, and very small when compared with that for mental illness in younger people (Lacro, Harris and Jeste 1995). Yet everyone who has worked in social work, general practice or community nursing will have encountered people whose symptoms suggest a psychotic disorder, and who pose a difficult management problem. Older people with psychosis seem to want to talk at length about their symptoms, but practitioners often find this difficult, especially if relatives are present (McCabe *et al.* 2002). Often the people who are left to hear about these feelings are home care staff, friends and family. How might they respond? Should they:

- 'prove' that the feelings are delusions and imaginary?
- 'go along' with them?
- distract the older person, for example, by changing the subject?

Practice example: Mr H, aged 77

Mr H visited the housing department frequently to complain how depressed he was about his housing, which was infested with fleas. He could not stay in the house for more than a few minutes before becoming unbearably itchy all over, and so spent as much time as possible travelling on buses and trains, even during the night, with his important possessions in plastic bags slung over his shoulder. His daughter – who was not affected in the same way when in his flat – nevertheless had it fumigated several times. Mr H was also preoccupied with gum disease, and went from dentist to dentist to get cures, although none of them were able to identify any such disease.

Learning points

Although Mr H says he is depressed he is actually driven by two delusions, one of which he attributes to the flat, and the other of which is hypochondriacal, for he has no gum disease. He does not have other depression symptoms (see Chapter 1).

Treating him as depressed will not change his symptoms or alleviate his problem, but use of an anti-psychotic medication may well help, as may him moving home.

Moving home may need to be addressed and managed carefully, through a balance of the risks, let alone the practicalities. Involvement of the housing department may be best if done early and with time to address all of the questions.

Mr H's daughter will need support because her concern for her father may have been difficult to express and sustain. His condition is not one that attracts a deal of sympathy or empathy; she may find it difficult to discuss his needs and her own feelings.

Practice example: Mrs Y, aged 85

Mrs Y believes that people get into her flat while she is out shopping or visiting friends, and interfere with her possessions, re-arranging the furniture, partially closing curtains and re-arranging clothes in her wardrobe. All this happens despite the locks that she has fitted, both on the main door to her flat and on the room and wardrobe doors. She cannot explain how people get in, but she knows they do, and so whenever leaving her home she takes important things that she does not want disturbed with her in a shopping trolley. So far, this is not attracting too much public attention but local youths are picking up the fact that she is behaving strangely and there has been some anti-social behaviour directed at her, such as spitting and name-calling. As far as she is concerned the problem is an external one, but is nonetheless very disabling for her, making her anxious and gloomy.

Learning points

Mrs Y is unhappy, but also has a 'partition delusion', and should be treated as having a late-onset psychosis, not depression.

Those working with Mrs Y need to be told what is happening and given support in managing their responses to her accusations.

Local community safety personnel, such as the neighbourhood community safety officer or police, need to be told that she is known to social services and who to call if they suspect that she is being harassed or victimized.

Mrs Y is a vulnerable adult and may be at risk of abuse. This may mean that if the situation escalates, individuals begin to think about whether their responses and care planning might be addressed within the context of adult protection in order to bring agencies together and to share information.

It is hard to keep the confidence of the older person with delusions, without colluding with them, but this needs to be the aim of the dialogue between professionals and the affected individual. Help should be offered, not to 'cure' the delusion, but to support the person made so anxious about it. We do not pretend that this is easy, and the best that can be achieved sometimes is an agreement to differ.

As the population ages, more older individuals will come into contact with front-line social and health care practitioners, expressing delusions, hallucinations or marked hypochondriasis among a wide range of other symptoms. The boundary between multiple physical complaints in an individual who does have arthritis, chronic lung disease and depression, and the overwhelming preoccupation with bodily symptoms which fit no pattern in the hypochondriacally deluded older person may sometimes be difficult to discern, explaining why referral to medical specialists and admission to hospital for investigations are common for this group.

Psychosis in old age often needs specialist attention, both for diagnosis and for treatment, but its nature may prevent or delay specialist referral, especially when paranoid features are present in the illness. The social worker or general practitioner confronted with it needs to understand the essentials of late-life psychoses, in order to inform and advise families, brief other agencies working with the older person and seek appropriate specialist support.

General practitioners and social workers faced with older people who develop delusions, hallucinations and hypochondriacal preoccupations therefore need to think about:

- the previous ('pre-morbid') personality of the individual, using informant histories wherever possible to supplement their own knowledge and records

- any previous history of psychiatric disorder, particularly 'breakdowns' or prolonged hospital admissions in earlier life that might be signs of a psychotic episode or a major depressive illness

- current features of their thinking or behaviour that suggest cognitive impairment, particularly loss of functional ability, or emotional lability (tearfulness), as well as memory loss

- other complaints suggesting a depressive disorder, especially anhedonia – the inability to find pleasure in anything – or multiple physical complaints

- visual and hearing impairments, which are often undetected or underestimated by both older people, their social contacts and professionals.

There are five major psychoses that affect older people:

1. early onset schizophrenia in its late stages

2. late onset schizophrenia

3. delusional or paranoid disorders

4. psychosis in dementia

5. psychosis in depression.

In later life, early onset schizophrenia may affect up to one per cent of the population aged 65 and over (Gurland and Cross 1982). Nine out of ten of these people will have developed psychotic symptoms before the age of 45, and will represent the sub-group with schizophrenia whose symptoms remit or get better over time (McGlashlan 1986). Symptoms of schizophrenia may decline with age in this survivor group, and although social networks shrink (as with most of us as we age) the quality of relationships, coping mechanisms and practical skills may improve (Cohen 1990). A person who lives in a group home for people with mental health problems may, as the years pass, be finding life is getting better, with stronger links with friends and perhaps being able to re-establish relationships with family members, as well as acquiring better home-making and practical skills.

Paranoia as a symptom is more common than late onset schizophrenia, affecting four per cent of the population aged over

65, but may be associated with it or with dementia, and affects older women more than men. Paranoid symptoms are associated with previous personality disorder, hearing loss, immigrant status and low socio-economic status. There are also possible associations with physical or sexual abuse in early life, and not having had children (Gurian, Wexler and Baker 1992). Paranoia can be very dramatic, and bring the older person into conflict with family members, neighbours or the police. A study from Sweden suggests that older people with paranoid symptoms are often already known to social services, either because people's concerns about them have been picked up or because the older person is more prepared to accept some help from social services rather than help from family members (Forsell and Henderson 1998).

Discharge planning and the organization of aftercare for people with these kinds of problems can be complex, and the earlier they start the better. Although the care programme approach does not apply to older people in most areas, the systematization of follow-up that it requires is a useful model for community care of older people with psychoses.

About one third of patients with Alzheimer-type dementia develop psychotic symptoms, particularly persecutory delusions and visual rather than auditory hallucinations (Cooper *et al.* 1991). Persecutory and hypochondriacal delusions within a depressive disorder occur in only 1 per cent of those over 65, while 20 per cent of this age group has some depression symptoms, but delusions are associated with greater severity of depression and higher likelihood of referral to psychiatrists and admission to hospital (Katona 1994). In this area we are likely to come across that small number of older people who may be subject to the Mental Health Act 1983, either in respect of their compulsory admission for assessment and treatment, or in the community where legal powers (guardianship) grant access to professionals, require attendance (such as to a day centre) or require a person to accept accommodation. In considering this process, the professional needs to consider the effect on the relationship with

Practice example: Mrs Z, aged 88

Mrs Z had come to the UK from eastern Europe in 1956. She was something of a recluse, but a neighbour who had been distressed by her behaviour contacted the local social services department, triggering a visit from her general practitioner and, eventually, compulsory admission to hospital under the Mental Health Act 1983. She would, from time to time, go into her garden, or into the street, and shout abuse at her black neighbours or at passers-by. Her language was offensive, and the social work assessment noted her uncompromising and voluble racism as a major problem. Most of the time she barricaded herself into her home, which she occupied alone, refusing to let anyone in. Her husband had died some 20 years previously, and she had no children. This resistance to visitors eventually decreased when she was promised help in dealing with the persecution that she was experiencing. In her home there was little food, no heating, little evidence of cleaning and much long-term neglect of the building itself. She was convinced that her neighbours were able to get through the wall and damage her property, turning off the heating and electricity and trashing her rooms. Treatment at home with anti-psychotic medication made little difference and she ultimately required in-patient care.

Learning points

Mrs Z has a number of risk factors for psychosis, including migrant status and childlessness. She is distressed but not depressed by the persecution, which again takes the form of a 'partition delusion' flavoured by (probably long-standing) hostility to black people.

Those working with Mrs Z need to know about her offensive behaviour and to have support in dealing with it and with any effects on them.

Mrs Z may find it helpful to talk to someone in her first language and interpreting should be available for both the community based assessments and in the in-patient unit.

Religious and cultural issues, as for all older people, need to be considered. A group for older people from eastern Europe may be useful in providing support when Mrs Z leaves hospital but care will be needed in making sure that the group is one where she will feel comfortable.

Housing issues will need to be addressed, both in making sure the home is safe but also in making good the repairs and perhaps making the home more suited to Mrs Z's needs and any disabilities. Involvement with a specialist home improvement agency should begin as soon as possible to set such discussions and plans underway. A benefit check will likely be part of this process.

the older person but also the effects of such actions on relatives, who under the legislation are able to ask for an assessment or request a review of their relative's detention.

Confidentiality is sometimes difficult for all when there is psychotic illness in older people, sometimes at the first encounter when relatives or neighbours may be the ones who alert social services to the problem, and always during the process of continuing care, because they need to know how to understand the behaviour of the older person, how to monitor change and how to respond. While confidentiality is not overruled, except in extreme situations where there is a risk to the individual or others, the duty of care that professionals have to both the ill individual and the wider community means that both rights to information and confidentiality must be addressed. Recent guidance from the Royal College of Psychiatrists (2004) about information sharing advises that carers are given general factual information about the diagnosis, medication, services and support groups, and are helped to understand the restrictions on confidentiality. Carers should also be given the opportunity to see a professional on their own and to have an assessment of their own needs if they are providing substantial regular care, or this is envisaged. We return to carers' needs again in Chapter 7.

CHAPTER 6

Suicide and Self-harm

One of every eight people who commit suicide is aged 65 years or over. Men aged over 75 years have the highest rate of suicide among any age group. High and rising rates of suicide among older people – particularly men – are occurring worldwide (World Psychiatric Association 1999). If we can understand why people kill themselves we may be able to help them avoid suicide as a solution to their problems although the increase in suicide rates may be hard to stop as depression in younger people also continues to grow. In England and Scotland, strategies to prevent suicide are emerging, with implementation groups addressing problems at local levels (Department of Health 2002; Scottish Executive 2003) and national studies of suicide prevention in the general population and among groups at different life stages (McLean, Platt and Woodhouse 2004).

In England about 5000 people of all ages take their own lives each year, and in the four years between 1996 and 2000, the deaths of 20,927 people from suicide or open verdicts/deaths by undetermined causes were reported to the National Confidential Inquiry for England and Wales (Appleby 2001). For Scotland, the figures for the three-year period between 1997 and 2000 were 2650, and over the same period in Northern Ireland the figures were 502 people. Table 6.1 draws out the figures by age groups for England and Wales from the Inquiry; for Scotland and Northern Ireland, see Appleby 2001.

Table 6.1 General population suicides over four years 1996–2000
(England and Wales) by age and gender

Age	Men	Women
55–64	1661	643
65–74	1126	628
75 and over	1178	736

Source: Appleby 2001

**Box 6.1 Key findings in 200 cases of suicide
by older people in Cheshire 1989–2001**

- Gender plays an important part; men are more likely to commit suicide but are less likely to be known to the psychiatric services and have less reported history of a prior attempt.

- A large proportion of people who commit suicide have had no recent contact with heath services.

- Outreach services may be the best way to contact people who do not use social services.

- Eighty per cent committed suicide apparently on their first attempt.

(Source: Salib and Green 2003)

Multiple reasons underlie suicide, although there may be a single trigger. Not everyone who commits suicide is depressed, but as Wolpert (1999) describes from his own experience, suicidal thoughts can be overwhelming at times: 'When I was at my most depressed I thought of little else' (p.64). Most older people who commit suicide have had recent contact with their general practitioner (about one third in the preceding week) and most have had major depression, though some do not appear to have signs of any problems. As Box 6.1 shows, from analysis of coroners' inquests in one part of England over 13 years, there are some common themes but also differences among those older people who commit suicide. It should be noted, however, that this study looked at records where there was a verdict of suicide. Some other studies of suicide argue that it is appropriate to look at a broader range of deaths, such as those where the verdict is open or non-accidental.

Suicide risks

The following factors indicate higher risk of suicide:

- Demography: older age and male gender, especially older men aged over 80 and people who are isolated; physical illness (see below) seems to be more important as a trigger for suicide in older men than in women (Quam and Arboleda-Florez 1997).

- History: a history of previous attempts, evidence of planning such as making a will, a recent bereavement. However, most older people who kill themselves have not made a suicide attempt before, making a will is logical and sensible, and bereavement is common and normal.

- Physical factors: chronic and painful illness or disability, alcohol misuse, abuse of sedatives or hypnotic drugs such as Nitrazepam or Temazepam seem to be factors that explain suicide in some older people. In physical illness, pain seems particularly significant (Cattell 1988). Much seems to depend on the meaning of the physical problems for the individual and whilst intractable pain is undoubtedly depressing, depression can alter the experience of pain as well. Proud but rather rigid individuals who would rather not live if unable to do so with their normal vigour may opt for suicide, especially if depressed mood biases their judgements about the implications of their illness (Snowden 2001).

- Mental state: in-depth interviews with people who knew a person who had committed suicide and were in contact with them immediately before their death, suggest strongly that 90 per cent or more had diagnosable mental health disorders. The manifestations of these include: suicidal thought, plans of suicide, marked agitation (someone who is obviously restless and feels inwardly restless), profound hopelessness, feelings of worthlessness, guilt or self-reproach, marked insomnia, marked hypochondria (excessive worry about illness), psychotic ideas (such as feeling persecuted). Depression is commonly associated with suicide but there is a puzzle here. Depression states fall with older age, and women are more likely than men to experience severe depression, but men are more likely to commit suicide.

Analysis of coroners' records for 210 older people who committed suicide in Sydney, Australia (Snowden 2001), showed the following patterns:

- 25 per cent of older people were depressed in response to losses, including bereavement.

- 24 per cent of older people were 'understandable' suicides because they wanted to end their physical suffering (from cancer or degenerative neurological disease, such as motor neurone disease), or to relieve a perceived burden on others. However, nearly two thirds of this group were also depressed.

- 18 per cent of older people had a depressive illness without obvious external cause, and some were deluded (for example, they thought they had a terminal illness when they did not).

- 13 per cent of older people were in situations which they experienced as untenable, like financial ruin or guilt.

- 10 per cent of older people were depressed following worsening of their health, or of a disability.

- 6 per cent of older people had either dementia or a psychiatric illness (see Chapter 4 for further discussion of dementia and Chapter 5 for psychosis); in three quarters of these people depression symptoms were present.

- 4 per cent of suicides in older people proved difficult to explain.

This study shows how complex the problem of suicide in later life can be and how difficult it may be to prevent. The characteristics of those at risk of taking their own life are hard to pin down. Most severely depressed older people do not commit suicide, even if significantly disabled, so probably the group that should attract the concern of GPs, community nurses and social workers most of all is that of older men living alone whose lives are changed for the worse by illness or disability. The problem is, of course, that they are often the group least likely to be in regular contact with health or social care services.

Studies of what seems effective in averting suicide are less common than those analysing its causes, but interviews with people about what helps when they feel suicidal provide some clues. Eagles *et al.* (2003) report that they consider a variety of contacts supportive. These include access to psychiatric services, their relationship with social and religious networks and self-help groups. The stigma of mental illness makes their problems worse.

The story of Mrs F develops some of these risk factors into a practice example to draw out some of the complications of working in a situation of uncertainty.

Practice example: Mrs F, aged 74

Mrs F visits her GP on the prompting of her solicitor who thinks she could do with a 'bit of a check up' as she is not her usual self. Talking to the GP she complains of having very little energy after a recent bout of flu six weeks earlier. She has stopped going to church and to her bowls club. Physically she is well and all tests are normal. She does admit to feeling depressed and is guilty about this, and about wasting the doctor's time. She says she has had a good life and has a loving family, but starts to say that everyone would be better off if she were 'out of the way' as her family have their own lives to live. She agrees to take some anti-depressants but asks for something mild, as she is worried about side effects and becoming an addict. Her GP prescribes Lofepramine (70mg at night) and asks her to increase this dose after one week to 140 mg. She is not too happy about this, as she does not like taking drugs.

After one month Mrs F is no better, if not worse, and says when she returns to see her GP that she will never feel her old self again. He asks her permission to talk to her family and although she is a little surprised at this, and wonders if he is going to tell them something awful, Mrs F agrees. The GP arranges this quickly and continues to prescribe the medication but this time in small quantities and in the safest possible form. Talking to Mrs F's son on the phone, the GP finds out that her son and other relatives are also very concerned about Mrs F and worried about some things that seem ominous, such as her reluctance to talk about the coming Christmas arrangements with them. When the GP next sees Mrs F she is not any different but he suspects she is not seeing the point of coming to see him. The GP has a word with his colleague about his concerns and thinks that he might call the old age psychiatrist about Mrs F.

The next time he sees Mrs F, the GP is really concerned that she is a danger to herself. He asks her if she would be willing to see a specialist because he thinks her depression is getting worse and that it would be helpful to get some extra advice on the best way to help her. Mrs F refuses and does not turn up to her next appointment. The GP phones her and Mrs F thanks him profusely for his trouble in doing this but does not say she is alright and indicates that the doctor has many more people who he should be worrying about rather than her. Based on this, the GP decides to draw in colleagues from the mental health team, asks the approved social worker to call on Mrs F and talk further to her son who is also increasingly worried, especially since his mother has cancelled a proposed visit and seems 'very strange'.

When the social worker calls, Mrs F says all is fine but the social worker is very concerned about her and the state of her home. It seems to have been very well cared for but it now seems as if Mrs F has been doing a lot of throwing out and putting things in order. There is no sign of preparations for Christmas and the post looks unopened. Mrs F's son phones the social worker to ask what is happening and says how all this is very out of character for his mother. The social worker has worked with the GP before and feels that probably Mrs F has received all the help on offer locally and that something more needs to happen. This view is strongly confirmed when Mrs F admits that she has actually stopped taking the medication but hasn't told the 'nice doctor' as she thinks he would be cross with her for wasting his time.

The social worker talks further with the GP and the nurse manager at the mental health unit for older people. She suggests to Mrs F that it might be time for her to have a stay in hospital, as she is obviously not feeling her normal self and that people are worried about her. Mrs F is adamant that she is not going anywhere and that she will have nothing more to do with the social worker or the GP. The social worker completes the necessary forms for the admission of Mrs F for assessment under the Mental Health Act 1983 because she is convinced that Mrs F is a danger to herself and will now not co-operate with any assessment or treatment in the community. Mrs F is taken to the mental health unit by ambulance and the social worker makes sure that all the practicalities of the house are being dealt with by her family.

Mrs F goes into the assessment unit, and more history is taken from her about how she is feeling and what medication she has been taking, her eating and how she has been managing. Her key nurse explains her rights to her and the psychiatrist who sees her suggests she tries out some new medication (Fluoxitine). The nurses observe her and try to involve her in some of the unit's activities, but initially Mrs F decides to keep to herself.

In three weeks time, the medication appears to be having some effect; Mrs F is visibly less anxious and has been joining in some of the unit's groups, such as the painting sessions and cooking club. She has started to watch TV with some of the other patients and to join in the occasional game of cards. She is also becoming more talkative and says how well she feels. She is taking her medication without cajoling and seems to be almost comfortable in the unit.

After a stay of six weeks, Mrs F goes home with a plan of care that means she will receive regular visits from a community mental health nurse and has her phone number if she feels she wants to talk to someone. She goes back to her GP for a repeat prescription and talks to him about how ill she has been and how much more like her old self she feels. Over the following months, the community nurse visits less frequently; Mrs F starts going back to church and her bowls club and joins a social group to improve her new-found skill at cards.

Her medical records will show that Mrs F has received treatment as an in-patient for severe depression and this informa-tion may be available to others who support her for any physical problems she might face in the years to come. She appears to have responded well to the support she received, but it is not clear why. If she becomes unwell again then she and her family may be better equipped to know that services are available and what might be warning signs of relapse. How long will Mrs F keep taking her medication? The answer to this is uncertain but she may stop again with the knowledge and support of her GP to ensure there are no issues with withdrawal.

Learning points

We have presented this case study to illustrate a number of points. The first is that listening to Mrs F was important, for example, in identifying her increasing sense of hopelessness. Conaghan and

Davidson (2002) observe that people who had attempted suicide seemed to be far less able to identify positive future experiences than other older people. In the case of Mrs F, both GP and social worker looked out for a changed and worsening mental state, and this too was the role of the community mental health nurse who visited Mrs F when she returned home. All of them conveyed the importance of these to Mrs F and to her family. The second was the ability of the GP and social worker to compare Mrs F's current situation with her former behaviour and that they were able to contact her family. How might such a case have been handled if family were not there? Like many such examples, we will never know whether Mrs F was going to harm herself, but the risks were identified and assessed by the practitioners (for further details of the English legal framework see the Social Care Institute for Excellence 2004). We next consider risk in more detail.

The case of Mr Frederick Joseph McLernon, aged 81

In 1997 Mr McLernon took his on life on the railway. Mr McLernon lived in Antrim, Northern Ireland, and the Social Services Inspectorate (SSI) (1998) conducted an inquiry into his death. This inquiry is one of the few that offers multiple perspectives on the suicide of an older person. What can we learn from it to help practice? Three key sets of questions emerge:

1. The risk that community care assessments can miss possible indications of mental health problems and suicidal intent. In this case a social worker and district nurse undertook a joint comprehensive community care assessment. This assessment did not confirm that Mr McLernon met the eligibility criteria for nursing home care (Mr McLernon wished to enter a particular home for ex-servicemen). Why was he so insistent on this? What lay behind his refusal of home care support?

2. In this case a formal risk assessment was not carried out, although Mr McLernon was a frequent visitor to the social work service and had been referred by his GP and a voluntary organization. Should more efforts have been made to conduct a more thorough assessment, involving other professionals? Should a case conference have been held?

3. How can individual practitioners make use of supervision to reflect on their practice and the decisions they have made? How can those working with older people create opportunities for supervision and training when work is accumulating? How can organizations invest in this area in the face of competing demands?

Mr McLernon's death was violent and tragic. Unlike many other suicides it prompted an inquiry. As the Confidential Inquiry (Appleby 2001) observes, these have the capacity to help services think. But, as in this instance, they can also reveal the difficulty of engaging with older people who are potentially in distress but who seem to be clear about what they want and uncompromising (see also Conn and McVicker, 2000).

Reducing the risk of suicide and self-harm

Advice on reducing the likelihood of suicide comes from a variety of sources. The Social Service Inspectorate report on older people with mental health problems living alone, for example, Barnes (1997) suggests that all agencies need to be alert and should therefore have good links so that risk factors are known to all practitioners and warning signs can be identified. A review by O'Connell *et al.* (2004) advocates more rigorous screening. Minimizing access to the means of suicide may be something that staff should try to do, such as spotting that an older person is accumulating supplies of medication (the most common method of suicide among older women is an overdose of prescribed drugs).

Shah *et al.*'s (2002) study of suicide by drug overdose among older people in England and Wales over a six-year period shows that the most commonly used drugs were paracetamol and paracetamol-based compounds. They advise that these, along with anti-depressants and benzodiazepines, are prescribed with caution.

In an important study from Sweden, Rutz *et al.* (1989) report what happened after a community-wide approach to the prevention of suicide through an intervention directed at GPs. All GPs on an island in Sweden received education about suicide risks and depression in later life. Following this, suicide rates on the island were found to have declined when compared to the rest of Sweden (they had been the same for the previous 17 years). While this may not be conclusive, the study suggests that such education and training are partially effective. From Italy comes an example of a longer term support service for older people who were provided with a telephone helpline and advice line (De Leo, Bruno and Dwyer 2002). The number of suicides, especially among older women, decreased over an 11-year period.

Interest in constructing lists of risk factors which can inform preventive strategies lies behind many risk assessment policies, but like many of these documents the process of collecting information about risks needs to be placed in the context of decision making. Death by suicide is an event with profound consequences, both for the individual concerned and for those affected by it. But it is also a rare event. *The National Suicide Prevention Strategy for England* (Department of Health 2002) identifies older people as a high-risk group and commits itself to consultation around efforts to reduce this worrying trend. However, some are critical of the length of time this is taking, Seymour and Gale (2004, p.3) consider that suicide prevention among older people lacks 'any coherent approach' to the extent that the lack of such a strategy constitutes a 'scandal'.

Hepp *et al.* (2004) acknowledge the difficulty of collecting evidence about what works in preventing suicide among those who have made a previous attempt, but are hopeful that responses that keep channels of communication open may reduce people's sense of isolation and help them feel connected. This may help at a time of crisis and with seeking help. Provision of 'green cards' of emergency contacts and building up a trusted relationship (the therapeutic alliance) are some of the service developments suggested. Such 'lifelines' or 'anchors' the authors insist, must be real, and have someone at the other end.

Risk assessment in practice

There is less evidence about self-harm among older people than about younger people where the issue has been identified as one where services must develop a more co-ordinated and less 'blaming' approach. In many areas this has led to the development of services to support people who enter accident and emergency departments of hospitals for treatment, such as through liaison psychiatry posts held by consultants or nurses. These services are designed to provide early recognition of the problems and to ensure that there is follow-up of the individual once injuries have been treated. Studies of attempted suicide (such as that of Hepple and Quinton 1997, who report on a follow-up of 100 cases) suggest that older people who attempt suicide have a high mortality rate from later completed suicide and death from other causes. Even many years after an attempt, the risks remain heightened, as a study of what had happened to people 22 years after their suicide attempts illustrates (Jenkins *et al.* 2002). We indicate some of the difficulties of practice in this area with the example of Mr R.

Distinguishing deliberate self-harm from a suicide attempt is rarely easy and studies tend to show that the profile of those older people who attempt self-harm is rather similar to that of those who commit suicide (Nowers 1993). A study of older people in the London Borough of Tower Hamlets looks at figures for the years between 1978 and 1984 and identifies 102 cases of older people who had deliberately harmed themselves (Nowers 1993).

Practice example: Mr R, aged 72

Mr R, a retired farmer, has been discharged from hospital following treatment for a serious gunshot injury. He is adamant that this was the result of an accident with his shotgun; his wife is less certain and pours out her worries to the GP. She is particularly anxious because Mr R's father hanged himself and her husband appears to have been very depressed since his retirement. Mr R wants to 'put the accident behind him' and is very dubious about the value of seeing anyone, particularly a young nurse, let alone a social worker.

In this situation we feel that support for Mrs R is very important and that certain practical things might be done, such as trying to make sure that her husband has no access to guns. A risk assessment document might provide the basis of such identification. We suggest that while Mr R is not initially willing to see the nurse, that her visits to Mrs R may be very helpful and that Mrs R should be given advice about whom she should contact in a crisis and some ideas about how long help will take to arrive. In many areas, the assertive outreach service might become involved, or at least be able to give support to the older people's mental health team with ways to keep contact and build relationships with people who are 'difficult to engage'. We suggest that Mrs R should be encouraged to phone the nurse or GP with any queries and that the situation should be regularly reviewed.

Since, in this instance, it appears that Mr R's mental health was not assessed in hospital (contrary to recommendations), we suggest that this becomes a priority for the primary care team and that someone, such as the GP, takes responsibility for talking with Mr R and asking him directly about whether he feels like harming himself, if so, what plans he has made, and what might stop him from doing so. Asking people directly about their intentions is now seen as acceptable, rather than as previously when it was believed that to ask about suicide might give people the idea. This is suggested to family members too, who should 'probe gently' if they suspect that suicide is being considered, through asking how deep the intention may be and whether previous attempts have been made or a specific plan is in mind (Battison 2004).

Almost all, 95, had taken an overdose, virtually all of this was of prescribed medication, and levels of physical ill health were high. About 40 per cent appeared to have had a history of self-harm. Although this study took place some time ago, it appears still relevant and the dangers of overdose remain evident.

Those left behind

The impact of suicide on those who are involved either personally or professionally is often immense and long lasting. While bereavement by suicide is not necessarily more severe than other types, stigmatization, shame and a sense of rejection are more common (Hawton and Simkin 2003).

Family members and friends left behind after a suicide face a heavy burden (Redfield Jamison 2000). Writing of the impact of suicide in the self-help literature, Rowe (2003) suggests:

> Every suicide is a message to the living. The person might leave a note saying, 'You'll be better off without me', but no loving message can hide the fact that suicide is a rejection of family, friends and the world. (p.61)

The ripples of the event can provoke feelings of blame and guilt, with practitioners moving away from work in this area or finding that their judgement is impaired. Employers and colleagues can be supportive but they may prove insensitive and suggest that practice has been inadequate and that the individual worker is at fault. Counselling or therapy for individuals, families or groups may be effective, although there is not yet much conclusive evidence (Hawton and Simkin 2003).

'Postvention' is a term that is used to describe approaches to stopping the ripples becoming overwhelming and attention to it can help those facing bereavement by suicide. For families the existence of voluntary sector self-help groups, such as Compassionate Friends (Shadow of Suicide) (for parents who have lost a child and siblings) and Survivors of Bereavement by Suicide

Practice example: The Laurels

The death by hanging in his bedroom of Mr W was deeply upsetting to the home's residents. Despite the inquest finding that no one was to blame, rumours grew. News of his death had spread rapidly among the staff, though the residents were never told what had happened but found out through the evening paper. The care assistant who found him was too upset to return to work and her wages were sent to her in the post with her termination of employment papers. The residents were appalled when his room was re-let immediately and they were told not to mention Mr W as it was too upsetting. They found that staff were now very inclined to disturb them when they wanted some peace in their rooms and that many were forgetting to knock before they entered.

Learning points

What might have been better practice? We suggest that the home's manager might have benefited from thinking through with her colleagues the best way to support residents, staff and herself at this difficult time. The home as a community might have found it useful to have held some ceremony in remembrance of Mr W; perhaps a local religious leader might have helped organize this and been available to staff and residents. We think that going to the inquest and giving evidence would be times when the staff concerned would have benefited from support from each other, and that supervision might help the care staff think about their anxieties – perhaps that they should have been more observant and not left residents in their rooms. Work with a trainer or the home's inspectorate might help the staff, including all those working in the home, such as the administrator, kitchen staff and cleaners. The anniversary of Mr W's death might also be a time when some staff or residents would find it useful to talk through their feelings and memories. All these suggestions are an attempt to help those who have responsibilities to those left behind to repair or limit the damage of a suicide.

(SOBS) may be important and lasting sources of support, together with local groups such as CRUSE Bereavement Care. They may be particularly helpful because of the continued stigma of suicide and its effect on those who are linked by association with someone who has committed suicide.

For organizations, thinking about immediate and longer term responses to suicide may be an important part of supporting service users and staff. These can include developing policies about what to do in the event of a death or serious incident. Such policies can include handling communications, support and involvement in the funeral and during the inquest process, and providing opportunities for supervision or debriefing for all those who have been affected. We illustrate this with an example from a care home on page 95.

Conclusion

The learning points from this chapter are that suicide is complex and that it is not always associated with depression. Findings that older people who took their own life were depressed, but that this was unrecognized, may seem to justify blaming professionals for having missed something. We hope to have shown that while some will have made contact with services prior to their death, their depression may not have been easy to identify and that hindsight is perhaps being used to explain why the suicide happened, in some search for meaning and even blame. The great majority of older people commonly experience all the factors that appear to be associated with suicide in later life. A search for simple risk factors is likely to give many 'false positives'. If we have scope to develop services, these might usefully lie in seeing whether support for people who have made a suicide attempt can be brought into the mainstream of health and social care, and in devising support for those 'left behind'. This is not to undervalue the role of suicide prevention but to point to our limited knowledge of what can support older people around this event. Greater ability to respond to depression may be the better path.

CHAPTER 7

Carers' Support

The *Forget Me Not* review of services for older people with mental health problems (Audit Commission 2000) outlined what carers and service users said they would find helpful: This included:

1. contact with and education for GPs

2. training and education for carers

3. information, advice and advocacy services

4. responsive services based on need that has been assessed

5. monitoring of GP referrals

6. link workers with specialist services.

We will use carers' own agendas provided above to organize this chapter, noting throughout that many of the calls for GPs to act or improve cannot be addressed without involving the whole primary health care team and social care partners, as well as colleagues from housing and hospitals, and communities themselves. We have added to this chapter points relevant to those working with depressed older people and carers. While there are clear differences between those who are paid to care and those who do so on the basis of family relationships or friendship, many of the demands and points made by carers are echoed by those working in the area. As we indicate, for example, in Chapter 2, depression affects family and practitioners, and as we observe in Chapter 6, family and staff bereaved by suicide may express similar feelings and needs. Finally, we know that many of those working with older people have or have had caring responsibilities and so there may be further overlap.

Despite the high numbers of older people with depression and the impact of the condition, as we outline in Chapter 2, there are surprisingly few studies of services for their carers, compared to those of carers of people with dementia (Arksey 2003). In a systematic review of 40 studies of educational and psychosocial interventions for people caring for relatives with dementia, Cooke *et al.* (2001) note that two thirds of the studies did not show improvements other than carers' better knowledge of the condition of dementia (an important gain, nonetheless). Seymour and Gale (2004) suggest, however, that more recent research indicates greater gains. In the UK there remains a need for interventions to be evaluated, and it seems that service developments, when and where they are researched, are often looked at in isolation. Such research will also need to address some of the apparent perplexities of evaluations, for example, that carers' groups are generally rated very highly by carers but do not always appear to 'make a difference' in health or well-being. Should we respond to this by continuing to support such groups or should we look to develop other services? Are we measuring the right 'things'?

Contact with and education for GPs

Being a carer is not a guarantee for developing a mental health problem but some carers do seem to find caring particularly difficult and may experience problems such as depression. We know that women caring for a relative with dementia, for example, have an increased risk of developing depression (Livingston, Manela and Katona 1996). We now know that Afro-Caribbean carers in London report feeling that their lives are more restricted and that they need more financial help than white counterparts (Koffman and Higginson 2003). However, it may not matter what type of problem the older person receiving care is experiencing. Depression can affect carers when they are supporting a person with other long-term conditions; Miller, Berrios and Politynska (1996) suggest that carers can be particularly affected by depression if they are supporting a person with Parkinson's who is depressed. They argue that treating the depression of the person with Parkinson's also may help the carer.

Murray *et al.* (1997) identify that caring for a spouse with a psychiatric illness results in a high rate of mental health problems among carers, and suggest that it is not so much the loss of a confiding relationship that occurs but the loss of the relationship itself. They argue that such carers may benefit from support that is tailored to their individual needs. A similar finding that some spouse carers may benefit from counselling, support and individualized consultation with a practitioner is reported by Jang *et al.* (2004) in New York, but they point to differences among spouses as some may have a tendency to persistent anxiety (neuroticism) that is hard to ameliorate. In other words, some carers may have pre-existing mental health problems that caring may contribute to or, of course, make no difference or even improve. The focus on the needs of spouse carers is relatively new (see Milne *et al.* 2001) and comes both from better understanding of this 'hidden' group and demographic trends that mean that carers in later life form a growing proportion of carers, often providing intensive care for many hours each week.

We need to think about caring across time rather than as a snapshot since it is rarely static, as we will discuss later. Following care giving, after the death of the person they are supporting, some carers may be seriously affected by the bereavement. There is evidence that particular problems may be found among carers who have received little social support while they are caring and find caring difficult (Schulz *et al.* 1997).

In light of these consistent findings that carers may become depressed while caring and that caring for someone who has depression is difficult, why is there continual reference to a lack of professional support and limited services? Some of the reasons why carers may find that their needs are under-recognized by practitioners, not only GPs, may be that professionals are unclear about their own role. Nolan, Badger and Dunn (1999), for example, argue from the basis of interviews with 50 front-line nurses that they may be finding that the increased focus on cognitive behaviour and other therapies reduces their confidence that they can help, and enhances their belief that psychologists may be more effective. In their view, nurses' confidence is low and roles are not clear, a situation that they recommend is remedied by more community based training, better and more extensive practice in assessment, access to supervision and the chance to spend time in many areas of practice.

In a similar vein, Firth *et al.* (2004) suggest that social workers generally concentrate on their 'value' base rather than evidence base in working with people with mental health problems and that their roles may need to be better defined at a time when there is more integrated working between health and social services. This greater definition of role is needed but in many ways roles will have to be flexible as people's experiences of depression are so complex and require tailored responses, including the ability to engage with an older person who may not want any help. Ideas about shared capabilities in mental health seem worth considering, especially when working with older people (Department of Health 2004).

We would suggest that the needs of carers with depression are under-recognized because they are often not assertive or able to identify what might help a seemingly intractable situation, without giving rise to increased guilt about their (in)ability to cope. Support groups for carers may seem difficult for depressed carers to use and professionals may seem centred on their relative rather than the carer. Help offered may set up further expectations that are difficult to meet if you are depressed, such as persuading a relative to be ready and on time for transport, to a day centre, for example.

In Chapter 2 we outlined the impact of caring for a relative or friend who has depression. It is evident that contact with a GP is an important route into services and that the local map of NHS, social care and voluntary sector services needs to be shared among the primary health care team, social care colleagues and wider public and voluntary services to alert all to what is available so that their advice to older people and their families is up to date and locally specific. Recent surveys by the Audit Commission (2004a) illustrate that many carers are not identified (or often not until crisis point) and that information is seldom passed to them. Education can be looked at rather narrowly as a matter of spotting symptoms and patterns more quickly and becoming better at this, but it also includes learning how to develop relationships with carers that mean they will be more likely to accept support. Shared learning can also be part of the process of jointly thinking about what is needed at local level and working out ways of making this a priority for service development. As we argue earlier, depression is not the most politically important of topics (unless linked to risk) and there are limited campaigning or pressure groups operating in this area for older people and their carers.

Training and education for carers

In recent years, training and education for carers has been delivered to carers, providing information about services, better ways of caring and explanations of the illness or disease. Many of these are based in services and led by professionals for a set number of sessions. While carers' groups may offer training and education to their members, social support is also a key element and many groups combine activities. It is evident that carers' groups are now very diverse and change over time. Mitchell (1996) reports that even in a small district of Glasgow, the six groups he studied varied by their type of organization (some sited in day centres, others in the community), by being generic (open to all carers) or by being specialist (focussing on one particular illness or condition).

Others may be united by similarities among their members, such as sexuality, ethnicity or 'stage' of caring (for example, a group for those with a new diagnosis or those who have been recently bereaved).

There is reason to believe that education may be what some carers want and what professionals feel confident in giving. As illustrated in Chapter 6 on suicide and self-harm in the example of Mrs F, individuals may hold views about the possible risks of medication that mean they cease taking it before it is fully effective and some feel that it is dangerous even to start. Carers who have received information about how and why medication may work may be able to support and advise relatives (Maidment *et al.* 2002). Interviews with 20 family carers reveal the extent of families' support with many aspects of medication, from the prompting and monitoring role and also with practical matters like collecting it, opening it and keeping it safe (Goldstone 1996). Some carers in this study discuss their routines but many report that it takes time to manage medication and makes them feel anxious. 'System irritants', like difficulties obtaining medication, inflexibility among pharmacists and health centres, and impenetrable packaging, are reported and some carers reveal having no one with whom they can discuss concerns about possible side effects. Home care workers, whose lack of time may add further pressure, may also experience these difficulties. Education may provide a forum for people to voice such concerns and can also provide support and ideas among carers about 'tips' and resources, but it is not the only way. Multiple sources of advice and peer support are likely to be effective in enabling people to receive information when they are ready for it and of a type that appears to be relevant to their unique circumstances.

In the previous chapter we explored the need to offer support to relatives such as Mrs R and the family of Mrs F. Services also need to acknowledge the vulnerability of those who have been bereaved from whatever cause, since some carers may find it difficult to adjust to life 'after caring', perhaps with reactions of extreme guilt or self-blame and they may be at risk of depression. Practice experience of helping the process of surviving the suicide of somebody close (Grad *et al.* 2004) suggests that both relatives, friends and practitioners may find it useful to talk to people outside their own circles (family, workplace), that acknowledging feelings may help people to cope with them, and that postvention practice is best if not prescriptive. Similar attention is needed for those whose relative has moved into a care home, perhaps evoking guilt in a carer that he or she has failed, or let his or her relative down.

Education for carers may be helpful but new emphases on carers as 'experts' (Nolan, Grant and Keady 1996) recognize that many have a depth of understanding and experience that means they know when they need help and what will work (see the example of Miss N below).

Practice example: Miss N, aged 78

Miss N has supported her widowed sister, Mrs L, for many years. The sisters enjoy each other's company and since Miss N lives in a small upstairs flat, she relishes the opportunity to share Mrs L's garden and being able to fuss over the family labrador. Mrs L's anxiety and depression are generally under control, but Miss N needs a brief hospital stay and seeks help for that period. Specifically, she would like someone who has been introduced to her sister to help with her medication, take the dog for a walk and provide some reassurance. Miss N feels that if she is not confident that these arrangements will be assured, then she will not be able to go into hospital. Such is Miss N's determination, that she is able to argue her case and surprises even the local professionals by somehow managing to get a care package in place exactly as she wants. No one quite knows how it happened in an area of resource constraints but Miss N has been quite clear about what she wants and is quietly insistent.

Information, advice and advocacy services

The poor take up of financial benefits by carers has been a subject of concern for many years and this should be addressed, not just because income is inherently important but because of the depression that seems to accompany poverty. Those who have been carers may face a legacy of poverty as their employment opportunities have often been curtailed and they may find resuming work difficult (McLaughlin 1994). Such risk factors for depression suggest the value of practitioners linking carers to financial advice and to sources of help around skills training and education. Carers' groups may address such matters and recent research into family friendly policies among employers indicates that some are developing workplace responses to carers that enable them to work flexibly (Audit Commission 2004a). Returning to the example of Miss N, when she was working she was able to arrange that her sister could telephone her at work and could get to the pharmacist during her lunchtime. Miss N, however, felt that she could not take up promotion or move to a job where there would be more travel. While she was working, there was no time to attend the meetings of the local carers' centre but she did find its newsletter kept her in touch with local activities.

Consultation with carers of older people with mental health problems in one area by Rogers (2000) identifies some of the challenges in work around service planning and delivery. For some family members, being a carer is not something they identify with, providing support by monitoring or encouragement may not seem like 'real work'. For many the boundary between the types of help they would provide, as a relative, is hard to distinguish between that undertaken by any husband, wife or close relative. While carers may be treated as a group, in fact they are very different in terms of relationship, their age, family circumstances, employment, geography and so on. We are also beginning to find out more about the many varied experiences of people from black and minority ethnic communities, including the range of needs, resources and experiences among them (see

National Institute for Mental Health England [NIMHE] 2004). Finally, many carers are likely to be disabled or in poor health themselves and so their situation is often 'fluid' (Rogers 2000).

In most areas, the availability of advocacy schemes is limited and although carers identify this as a need, many advocacy services focus on the disabled person, or are limited to specific conditions, such as learning disabilities or dementia (see Cantley, Steven and Smith 2003). This means that other organizations, such as local Age Concern or MIND groups, or professionals, may find themselves taking on the advocacy role or the carer is left 'battling' on their own. In the case of Miss N described above, much depended on how ready she felt to make enquiries about her situation and how she had been received in the past. National organizations may help put people in touch with local services or give them confidence to approach the right people; these include Carers UK and older people's organizations such as Age Concern, Help the Aged and the Relatives' Association. For those carers where the severity of the person's depression means that legal advice would be helpful, organizations like MIND may be able to refer people to local resources. While very few older people with depression are subject to the Mental Health Act 1983 (Dwyer 2003), the position of nearest relative means that family members may wish to have independent advice about their rights. This can also include finding out about help with managing financial affairs, such as enduring powers of attorney if the person with depression has set this up. New legal powers under the Mental Capacity Act 2005 may mean that relatives or a chosen person may have greater access to the legal system to help with financial and other decisions if the person they are supporting is not able to manage their own affairs.

Responsive to assessed need

Carers' assessments have been a central plank of service improvement, with rights to an assessment outlined in the Carers (Recog-

nition and Services) Act 1995 and the Carers and Disabled
Children Act 2000 establishing rights to an assessment from
social services, even if the person being cared for has refused to be
assessed. There is increasing evidence that such assessments
should be wide-ranging and structured. Guberman *et al.* (2003)
report that use of carers' assessment tools not only provides an
effective way of identifying what matters to carers but can also
impact on practice by revealing things that might be neglected
and identifying what is really important to an individual carer.
Such assessments can throw up further need but they may also
reveal areas where there is satisfaction, and how caring needs to
be seen in the context of a relationship. While, in theory, many
practitioners are well aware of such feelings, the focus on the burden of caring appears sometimes to overwhelm other more
rounded views.

Developing these ideas, the focus on outcomes has prompted
greater attention on what carers want from services, often both practical as well as emotional support. This may help services to be
more fine-tuned and to reduce the chance that services are offered
but then not taken up or discontinued because they do not fit
carers' routines or preferences. Such assessments may take more
time and while this is a problem it may make planning easier, particularly if they can be shared among agencies. Care management
has been much criticized for driving a formula based assessment
in which there is little time for assessor and carer to discuss and
reflect on the situation (Postle 2001). We await the evidence of
whether this will be improved by the introduction of a shared single assessment process. Meanwhile, the benefits of being clearer
about what is a desired outcome of a service should make assessments more focused, purposeful and concrete. This presents a
challenge to services if better assessments are to reveal what
is generally suspected: that older people generally have more
restricted access to services such as psychological support, help
with relationships and counselling, family therapy and mediation,
and cognitive behavioural therapy (Audit Commission in Wales

2004). Few older carers are offered such support and services are grossly under-developed, despite evidence that carers often find such help valuable. A study of older female carers who received educational support in coping with frustration found positive benefits (Gallagher-Thompson and de Vries, 1994) and this programme has been widely adopted in the US (Hepburn *et al.* 2003).

Arising from studies of people with schizophrenia, the role of relatives in prompting depression or not facilitating its recovery has been outlined by Leff (2001) in an overview of 'expressed emotion', a construct developed from psychiatry where the emotional functioning of family members and their relationships is seen to have an impact on a person's mental health and, importantly, can be changed for the better. The idea of working to reduce expressed emotion, to increase empathy and to change family's interactions has been applied to work with family members of depressed older adults (Hinrichsen, Adelstein and McMeniman 2004). Those who have completed the Thorn initative training may be able to offer some advice to colleagues in older people's services who wish to take this approach further, but practice experience is limited in many areas and professionals are in short supply to work in such ways with older people.

The advent of direct payments for older people and for carers means that some carers may be able to use money from social services to purchase their own social care (carers, of course, have often paid for services out of their own pockets). As yet we have few examples of this working and what carers might see as their priorities, but we can imagine that some carers may find this more flexible and use direct payments to tailor a service to their needs, for example, employing a person to accompany their relative on a social outing. In the case of Miss N, she might have been able to use a direct payments scheme to provide the type of help she wanted more intensively over a brief period and for it to be provided by a person whom the sisters knew and trusted. Miss N might also have been able to use such funding to scale down her commitment to such regular visiting of her sister and to re-establish some of her former interests. While direct payments could mean that Miss N would not have extensive contact with social services, their existence (after a process of assessment under community care systems and monitoring by social services) may mean that Miss N has greater confidence that social services may be able to provide further, appropriate and acceptable help in the future if her sister's condition begins to worry her or if her own health declines. The new Green Paper on adult social care may extend the role of direct payments (Department of Health 2005; Wistow 2004).

Monitoring of GP referrals

While monitoring of referrals is important to keep the needs of carers under review, what this also illuminates is the value of the 'carers as experts' model (described by Nolan *et al.* 1996) This is particularly relevant to caring for someone with depression, although it is usually seen in the context of dementia care (Nolan and Keady 2001). By setting it within the context of a relationship over time and through recognizing the difficulties of caring, this model acknowledges that many carers find their role rewarding and satisfying, at times, if not consistently. In the example of Miss N, we may imagine that the sisters have much in common and while Mrs L is very anxious and depressed at times, her sister has ways of coping with this. Mrs L's worrying, which a previous cleaning lady found so exasperating that she handed in her notice, is familiar to Miss N who knows how to 'switch off'. As Nolan and Keady (2001) point out:

> Experienced carers, many of whom have learned their skills and expertise by trial and error, often have a far better grasp of their situation than professionals, and acknowledgement of this is vital to a partnership approach. (pp.164–165)

In practice this means that an assessment approach that can discuss the quality of the relationship as well as identify practical needs is likely to result in a more fine-tuned plan of support.

While the single assessment process in health and social care may help draw together many different elements and perspectives, it may be that use of the Carers' Assessment of Satisfaction Index (CASI) (Nolan and Grant 1992) enables practitioners to have greater knowledge of what carers will see as 'good care' and therefore what they will see as acceptable. Nolan, Keady and Grant's (1995) study of the coping methods of 260 carers supporting relatives with dementia found they used a variety of strategies, such as managing events (getting information and help, talking over problems, relying on experience, forward planning and getting a routine). Information about how carers 'manage' their roles when caring for someone with depression is also important when negotiating between carers and the person receiving support about their possibly different views on the situation. At some stage a carer's assessment needs to be aligned and brought together with the assessment of the person who is depressed. Conflicts of interest or different perceptions of a problem or need may have to be faced. This may be when specialist services are able to provide a higher level of support than that available from primary care or care management services.

Link workers with specialist services

The development of specialist services for older people with mental health problems is uneven and patchy. In some areas, carers' workers exist to provide a route map to services, or to set up services for carers, such as groups, networks and improvements to existing systems. Examples that focus on reducing isolation and enabling greater social support (often seen as a way of reducing the possibility of depression in a general sense) include:

- Proactive work in health centres in offering carers a 'financial makeover': are they receiving all the benefits they are entitled to?

- A volunteer scheme to provide home visits to people with dementia to enable their carers to go out in the evenings, not to a carers' group in a day centre but for a meal and entertainment.

- A telephone network of carers in a rural area where regular 'conference calls' or two-way telephone conversations enable carers to provide mutual support.

Specialist support for carers can also attempt to make changes within services and more broadly, for example, by providing a vision of what a 'carer friendly' city/town/village might look like (see Box 7.1). As with other developments to foster older people's well-being and independence (Audit Commission 2004b), this means a wider acknowledgement that carers' needs are not confined to health and social care but have to be addressed by other public services, such as housing, planning, leisure and education. Similarly, employers need to consider their own responsibilities (and the advantage to the labour market) of providing a carer friendly workplace. Key to this appears to be the idea of 'flexibility' and a willingness to respond to what carers find useful rather than standard formula (Department for Trade and Industry 1999).

Carers' workers may operate as a specialist service but many of those in health and social care may see themselves also as specialists in carers' support. In dementia care, for example, the work of practitioners often centres on the support of family members, so much so that researchers point to the risk of professionals, such as nurses, being more inclined to listen and relate to carers than to the person with dementia (Adams and Bartlett 2003). We would argue that the support of family carers is a valid part of their work and that professionals need to manage the 'dual focus' of supporting people with a disability or illness and their carers. As Twigg and Atkin's (1994) research indicates, relationships between family carers and professionals can vary and may range from treating carers as fellow team members (co-workers), or as people with their own problems and needs (co-clients), or as the main providers of care (resources), or as needing to let go of their responsibilities (superseded).

Box 7.1 A 'carer friendly' town

What might a 'carer friendly' town, with an emphasis on the social needs of people with depression look like? It might include:

- a carers' centre with activities such as social groups, education 'tasters', computer workshops and so on

- agreement between the local advocacy schemes about their responses to carers

- family friendly policies supported by local trade unions, the Chamber of Commerce and carers' groups to provide confidence that carers in employment will meet with a sympathetic response

- access to transport concessions or free services when accompanying the disabled person

- publicity about sources of help/advice in public settings such as supermarkets, post offices and council offices

- well publicized concessions and support for disabled people and carers to cultural events and leisure services

- 'carer proof' policies and procedures among health and local authority bodies, i.e. that carers have been considered during regular consultations. These might include, for example, the protecting vulnerable adults policy, the charging policy for social services, the lettings policy of the social housing group and planned changes in the bus routes to the local hospital.

Does this mean that carers need specialist workers simply to access services or that professionals' views are one-sided and their practice does not inspire confidence among carers? We think that the complexity of caring in later life, and for people with depression in particular, requires instead a greater understanding by professionals of their needs, a greater focus on the skills required to support carers and better resources to bring in and make use of specialist help where it is needed. Carers of people with dementia have challenged professionals to improve practice in their area of concern: professional education has responded to this and has begun to make significant changes to services for carers. How can similar improvements be taken up in the area of depression?

CHAPTER 8

Prevention of Depression

Depressive disorders are the 'leading cause of disability world-wide' (Üstün and Kessler 2002). As we have argued in the previous chapters, the impact of depression is such that it frequently causes long-term disability and distress to older people and affects those supporting them, both family members and practitioners. Interventions work for some but not all and recovery may be only in part. The costs in human unhappiness are great. While older people are generally retired from employment, there are major costs associated with medical and social support as well as the loss of social capital, through the limits placed on older people's contributions to the care of their families and the well-being of their communities. This means that a focus on prevention is arguably where attention should be directed. In this chapter we outline some of the ways in which depression might be prevented, but also include ways in which depression might be prevented from getting worse and relapse avoided. There is not a large evidence base here and when prevention is discussed it is often in the context of prevention of suicide (see Chapter 6) and only to a limited extent even there.

This chapter looks at separate elements of prevention though their interconnections are obvious. They have a focus on the UK although we have much to learn from other countries and the clear messages that come from thinking about issues cross culturally and on a wider canvas. For example, the United Nations' revised Plan of Action on Ageing (2002) sets out a series of policy goals that have relevance to depression. These range from poverty reduction to strengthening support networks, development of primary health care services to recognition of the special needs of older people, support for carers and the reduction of stress and burden among women (Sidorenko and Walker 2004). From such a span of activity directed both at reducing vulnerability as well as improving support systems, it may seem a jump to consider the impact of individual 'triggers' but we would argue that this is a 'leap' that is worth taking.

What is prevention?

This deceptively simple question is highly relevant to depression. Do we mean strategies to prevent depression ever starting (primary prevention) or do we mean attempts to prevent it getting worse (secondary prevention), or prevent it from returning once treated effectively (tertiary prevention)? Is the real aim of any prevention strategy to reduce the use of costly services by depressed older people? Or are the purposes of preventive strategies to maintain and improve quality of life (Joseph Rowntree Foundation 1999)? If this is so, is it possible to single out depression from wider policy goals around health gain? Many health service models use ideas of primary and secondary prevention to make sense of such complexities. Primary prevention or preventability often focuses on causes or risk factors; secondary and tertiary prevention relate more to the prevention of disability in depression. All three elements are drawn together in the emerging prevention agenda.

Primary prevention of depression in later life would require two things. The first would be the reduction in the causes of vulnerability to depression, like loss of a parent in early childhood or lack of confiding relationships in early adulthood, over which we may have little control. The current generation of retired people have experienced both the traumas of the twentieth century and the benefits and relative affluence of the stable post-war period in Europe. Those in their eighties now grew up during periods of worldwide economic depression, mass migration of (mostly poor) populations and prolonged periods of warfare in which civilian populations were as much the targets of attack as the military. Those just retired grew up in the aftermath of that devastating period, with all its sorrows, and experienced the economic boom of the second half of the twentieth century. We cannot do much to change their characters and capabilities now, except to salute their resilience and support their efforts to remain independent at the end of their lives. We could think about how we might live so as to remain physically and psychologically well for the full length of our lives, but that is a separate story for another book.

The second approach to primary prevention would be mitigating the impact of adverse events in later life on an otherwise psychologically robust older person, for example, by controlling pain symptoms in someone with severe osteoarthritis of the hip joints, or relieving financial pressures, or by supporting them through bereavement, particularly when it is sudden and unexpected.

Practice example: Mr G, aged 82

Mr G described himself as a 'sprightly octogenarian' and enjoyed life. He had much to talk about, having travelled around the world as a young man, and having lived in several continents. He still liked to travel as much as his income permitted, but his enjoyable retirement was disrupted by the sudden and unexpected death of his younger brother (a mere 77 years old), from a heart attack. Mr G became immensely weary, and feared that he too was becoming ill. His doctor did lots of tests for diabetes, thyroid failure, anaemia, liver or kidney disease and heart disorders, but all were normal. The GP also talked with Mr G about his life, his brother (to whom he had been close) and his plans for the future. After three consultations, Mr G announced that he was feeling more energetic and was sure that his ill health had been because his brother's death had been 'out of turn'. He announced that he was planning to travel again, aiming for Damascus, because he had never been there.

'Unanticipated death syndrome' can include psychological shock, anger and even the persistent illusion that the dead person is still present (Newton 1988, p.143). For Mr G, early intervention addressing his physical concerns without neglecting his psychological state seems to have been beneficial, with rapid restoration of his stable mood and positive outlook on life.

Secondary prevention implies that coping strategies can be improved, so that adversity becomes easier to assimilate, using psychological methods to address negative thinking and low self-esteem. Biological symptoms of depression – sleep disturbance, slowing of thinking, loss of energy – can be treated with anti-depressant medication, to prevent depression becoming worse or an almost permanent feature of the person's life.

Practice example: Mrs Y, aged 69

Mrs Y thought that she had come to terms with her slowly worsening eyesight, and understood that its cause – a rare inflammation inside the eye – could not be eradicated but could be controlled. She needed to use steroids for this, which gave her a number of side effects, including osteoporosis, so she had to take extra medication to counter this. Her ability to manage everyday life worsened dramatically when a new neighbour became very troublesome, keeping her awake at night with loud music, and threatening her and her husband when they complained. A long process of investigation by the local council followed, and the home situation became increasingly difficult. Mrs Y began to dread the court appearance that she anticipated, and became tearful and unable to look after herself and her home. She lost weight, became agitated and could not sleep even when the neighbour was quiet. She began to see a counsellor based at a local voluntary sector group, who helped with her negotiations with the council as well as reframing her expectations of the court hearing from: 'It will be awful' to 'I will manage – if I have coped with being partially sighted I can cope with this.' She also started taking an SSRI anti-depressant, and slowly her mood stabilized and her agitation decreased. The noisy neighbour disappeared just before the court hearing, owing a lot of rent.

Tertiary prevention is designed to halt the recurrence of depression, or at least its deepening, in someone who has a long history of it. The prevention strategy may include long-term medication and carefully organized support from family, friends and services.

Practice example: Mrs Z

Mrs Z's family were frightened that she would starve to death. She was 77 and had lost her appetite so much that her weight fell from 57 to 42kg, and she became iron deficient. She was taken to see her GP by her worried daughter, and at first said very little, offering no account of what was happening to her and why she had stopped eating. No physical cause was found for her weight loss, and she reluctantly admitted that she might be 'a bit depressed'; her family said that she had always been 'a worrier'. To her GP's surprise she agreed immediately to the suggestion that she would benefit from a long course of anti-depressants, and came back to the health centre regularly to check her weight and iron levels, and talk with her doctor. Her weight started to rise after two months of treatment, she began to smile and talk, and her anaemia resolved. After six months of treatment her weight had stabilized at 49kg (still low for her height) and she said that her depression was 'almost gone'. She was offered, and accepted, long-term anti-depressant treatment, coming to the health centre every three months to monitor her weight and mental state.

We do not know why Mrs Z became so depressed, and if she knows herself she is not saying, but we can guess that she had in the past experienced much psychological distress, perhaps having recurrent depression masked by anxiety symptoms (see Chapter 5). By treating this serious and potentially life-threatening episode as one in a series of depressive episodes, a tertiary prevention approach with long-term medication and regular supportive reviews may have prevented a hospital admission for a very depressed and physically weakened individual.

Support is crucial to the management of depression in older people, but is poorly understood. It is sometimes confused with social relationships in an unhelpful way; one assumption being that social connectedness protects older people from depression. This belief comes from the observation that social isolation is associated with depression, but the seemingly logic belief that social connectedness will therefore function as an anti-depressant is not entirely supported by evidence. Social networks probably do protect people experiencing long-term strain – like chronic disabling diseases – but do little to offset the sudden losses and damaging changes that can precipitate a depressive illness. Effective support that probably has anti-depressant powers is regular, consistent, with a fair level of confiding but without being over-involved and critical (Newton 1988, pp.148–153). This is exactly what professionals working with older people can offer, particularly those who have frequent contact as home care workers, day centre staff or staff in care homes.

The prevention agenda

The White Paper *Caring for People: Community Care in the Next Decade and Beyond* (Department of Health 1989) shifted the emphasis of social care services to targeting more intensive support on older people with high levels of need in their own homes. Among these were people with depression and this shift clearly provided greater support to family carers as well as to individual older people. One decade on, there is increasing interest in the effect of this shift of focus on older people with lower levels of disability and the impact of the withdrawal of 'low level' support, typically the home help service (Clark, Dyer and Horwood 1998). Reductions in grant-aid to voluntary and community sector groups also suggest that their social support function was not always explicit or supported by evidence. This means that the debate on prevention has been caught up in a debate about low level services and, while the two are closely connected, they are not the same. Low level services are an intervention; prevention of depression is an aim. Low level services may not prevent crisis or 'excess' disability, and prevention may not be the outcome of a low level service.

However, it is not just a return to previous systems that is mooted, for there is little real evidence that such services were ever consciously oriented to prevention. The problems besetting older people lie in areas that cover both social care and health services but also range much more widely. Older people, it is argued, need greater or better information about what is already on offer and should derive this from single points of contact. Armed with such information, their access to services and community facilities should be less complex. Public services have a key role in these improvements and these arguments are encapsulated by influential policy discussion documents which promote 'inverting the triangle of care' (see Association of Directors of Social Services/Local Government Association 2003 and the series of reports issued by the Audit Commission 2004 a,b,c,d):

> The promotion of well-being and the development of preventative services for older people should be seen as a core function for all agencies. There should be a clearly identified budget for this core function, which should be determined at national level. (ADSS/LGA 2003)

The government appears to have responded quickly to this imperative with the Minister for Community returning the challenge:

> We know that low level preventative services can improve self-esteem and coping mechanisms and yet these early approaches are often resisted by people fearful of the consequences of being seen as needing support, everyone around you focussing on what you can't do and conspiring to run your life for you.
>
> You (social services) have to get across to the public, clearly and simply, what you do and how you can be used to improve their lives and lose the stigma that is still often associated with

> social services. You have to design pro-active services that stop problems happening and maintain independence not just services to pick up the pieces after the event and which lead to increased dependence. (Ladyman 2004)

Whether they are described as low level or low intensity, services that have prevention as their key aim face the challenges of working within a limited evidence base. This makes the financial shift as well as attitudinal realignments difficult in a climate of resource constraints. There is also continuing focus on hospital and acute services in the NHS, and in social care concerns about internal closures and the state of the care home sector overall. At local level, a 'think piece' from the Joseph Rowntree Foundation (1999) set out what it thought were the conditions for the development of prevention within services, particularly social care:

- cross agency and cross sector commitment
- engaging older people in service design and delivery
- locally based initiatives
- agency commitment at senior level
- dedicated budgets and staff (although there was a prevention grant, this was time limited but appears to have been taken up into mainstream services).

Nonetheless, such low level services, often hard to define and hard to cost, centre mainly on the NHS and social care arena while the prevention agenda might be more usefully taken out into other public services. Quilgars' (2000) literature review of low intensity support services and their effectiveness in three areas specifically included tenancy and housing support services, practical support services to increase social well-being, and schemes to reduce isolation through befriending. The span of these makes it evident that if we only focus on social care services, this will miss those who might be supported while at risk of depression, that is before they are identified as possibly needing responses from health or social care. If this is so, then public health information about depression needs to be taken into training for most of those working with older people.

Nolan (2001) suggests that preventive and rehabilitative care is in danger of becoming the 'new panacea' and so our final point in this section is one of caution. We know little of what works in prevention and have much to learn. Rather than waiting for clinical or best practice guidance, we can work carefully in practice, recording what we do and what happens, talking about it in supervision, and reflecting on ideas with our colleagues, particularly from other organizations.

Preventing depression in everyday practice

The earlier case studies hint at ways of approaching the prevention of depression through existing services and agencies. We also need to place this agenda in the context of health promotion for older people. Here we come across debates about exercise, activity and lifestyle changes. Many of these acknowledge that this area of science is under-developed.

This search for *risk factors* is often seen as a search for ways to respond to or even eliminate the 'triggers' that may place a person at risk of depression. Common triggers for older people are not much different than for other people, but triggers such as retirement or bereavement are more likely to be experienced in later life. More than 20 years ago, Murphy (1983) argued that since treating depression is not always effective we need to pay more attention to prevention, and that because severe life events seem to be so important as triggers then perhaps we should strive to lessen their effect. Similarly, she proposed that treating physical illnesses earlier may reduce the likelihood of people developing depression in response to these and that this area should be more widely considered because of the effect of such problems on other people. For example, support for those whose partner or family member has a major illness may be worth exploring since this stress has been identified as important among older people experiencing depression (de Beurs *et al.* 2001). The onset of anxiety is most likely when a partner develops a serious illness.

What might such support look like? We suggest that there are two service developments that might be worth considering as illustration. The first is to link early identification and diagnosis of physical or mental health problems to services that are able to respond to people's emotional and psychological needs when bad news is broken, and in the time afterwards when adjustments have to be made and fears faced. This means that people should not be left with 'bad news' and that the process of diagnosis should be seen as part of a system of support, rather than vague indications that support might be available and that leaflets might help. In the example of the early diagnosis of dementia, for example, we now have evidence of how many elements of a support system need to be in place for a response to be effective and supportive. These include, for example: support groups for individuals, counselling, individual and tailored information, membership of carers' groups and family networks, involvement in campaigning and research, access to specialist help and information, assistance with practical, legal and financial matters, etc. (see Chapter 4). Support that is more psychologically based, such as counselling and support groups, at the moment have greater evidence of their efficacy, and we have drawn attention to some of the implications for practice in Chapter 7.

Our second suggestion relates to bereavement, as in the example of Mr G, discussed at the start of this chapter (page 115). This is so common in later life that it is hard to see it as a 'trigger' for depression and if we did so we might be placing older people in a category of permanent vulnerability. But if, as the evidence suggests, the death of someone important or an accumulation of deaths might trigger depression in some individuals, what skills are needed to offer protection or support as an alternative to having to engage quickly when a person is showing signs of depression rather than the grief that might be seen as 'normal'? In many cases there are those with the skills and the ability to contact people in such circumstances. Primary care teams, for example, will know many of those who have been supporting older people who have died or who are being cared for at home. Both the NHS and social care may have a proactive role in contacting people who have been caring for someone to provide support if this is needed, or help with keeping or picking up social contacts. As we discussed in Chapter 7, carers' incomes may be low and even lower once the person they have been supporting has died. Widows' and widowers' groups (and similar for bereaved partners of same sex relationships) may offer significant support. Commitment is needed by public services to foster and sustain such groups if they are working well, or have potential but their membership is small or the group is facing difficulties. The existence of infrastructures in the community and voluntary sector may be effective in providing such support and a better alternative to NHS and social care managers or practitioners 'reinventing the wheel' by creating new, dedicated and often unsustainable services. We will expand on this theme of optimizing existing practice and provision in the concluding chapter.

CHAPTER 9

Conclusion

It may seem strange to end a book on depression in later life by arguing that the problem and responses to it need us to take a life-course perspective. In other words, we believe that many of the triggers and causes of depression relate to people's accumulated resources, both in terms of how they have learned to cope with adversity and how their networks and relationships support them. Thinking about depression using a social model rather than a medical one, and perceiving it primarily as a disability and only secondarily as a disease, allows us to link what people have learned earlier in life to the ways services and systems of care for older people function. A narrow focus on mental health in later life, typified by an exclusively medical model of depression, will have limited impact and effect, because it does not build on positive mental health promotion earlier on in life.

We are not arguing for a transfer of resources away from other population groups, such as younger people, to older people. The bidding system for resources within health and social care often looks like an exercise in robbing Peter to pay Paul, and many who work with older people feel it favours the youngest, less stigmatized and most attractive, or vocal. Resources for responding to mental health problems in later life in the UK are far from sufficient. There has been much attention to ageism within health and social care (Help the Aged 2002), and the inequalities this reveals are evident in mental health services for later life. Professionals are often scarce, this area of work is undervalued and champions to promote mental health in old age are few. What we do advocate is an investment in people that will allow mental health problems to be prevented or pre-empted where possible, and to be more easily identified and addressed when they occur. Some of this orientation of services needs to be towards the origins of depression in early life, and other parts of it lie in creating supportive environments as well as therapeutic interventions.

We draw together the main themes of this book by exploring possible frameworks for developing such an orientation. These are designed for those 'inside' each service or discipline to use to assess their own organization's or profession's ability to respond to the needs of older people with depression. They are also designed for those inspecting, commissioning or funding activities so that they can think about specific outcomes and approaches that they wish to support. Finally, we see these frameworks as potentially relevant to older people, their families and support or survivor groups in clarifying what they might wish to see in a locality, as a professional response or in a care provider. Public involvement in health and social care may be at early stages but both systems are more ready to consult each other, and some local involvement and participation strategies may help services to refine their approaches. Figure 9.1 is a schematic way of representing our framework.

Primary care organizations and local councils

We have grouped these together because of their key roles in promoting public health and well-being. While much work on mental health issues may be seen to be the responsibility of social services or social work departments, local authorities as a whole have key roles to play in promoting support in later life. In respect of prevention of depression, for example, we argue in the previous chapters that social support is important in preventing depression from getting worse. Social support is certainly less stigmatizing if

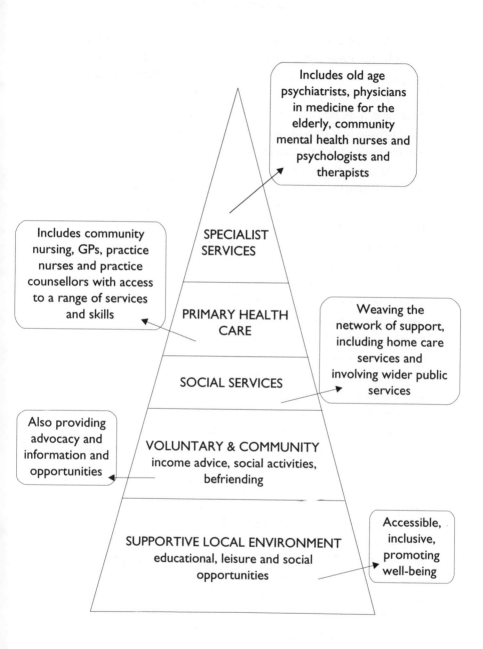

Figure 9.1 A system for preventing, managing and treating depression

it is provided outside a 'social work' or 'mental health' setting and through, for example, educational activities, leisure services, or artistic or creative activities. This means that a first question for primary care organizations like primary care trusts and local councils is how far they are investing purposefully in services for older people that provide (consciously or not) some level of support to those with depression. At its most simple this may involve financial support for the broad voluntary and community sectors with explicit acknowledgement of their role in social befriending, low level services and contact with those who are at high risk of depression, or who are depressed.

We know that not all voluntary sector groups are able to be explicit about their activities but discussions about how to identify such activities are likely to be fruitful. Cattan's research (2002), for example, on voluntary sector schemes that sought to address social isolation found that some were able to offer evidence of what they were doing by indicating the criteria for involvement and the aims of their service. Recent interest in low level support (see, for example, Audit Commission 2004b) may also signal greater willingness to adopt a preventative approach. The use of sport, leisure and cultural services by older people may be an important element in prevention and older people's groups can be effective monitors of the accessibility of such settings for older people. As some research on the regeneration of inner cities notes, for example (Scharf *et al.* 2002), older people do not necessarily feel that new facilities are welcoming to their age group.

Second, and more relevant to local social care and primary care organizations in their partnership working, or within emerging integrated care systems, are commitments to professional development that will provide the range and level of interventions we describe in Chapter 3. While social care is largely provided through organizations other than social services or social work departments, professionals such as social workers and occupational therapists, together with primary care colleagues such as community nurses, are weavers of the networks of support available to care staff, families and older people themselves. They carry out assessments and prompt agreements about and funding of care 'packages'. Any employing agency needs to invest in their professional development, through involvement in workforce development consortia and through negotiations around the content of training at pre and post qualifying levels. Audits of such training should establish whether depression is addressed as a topic, whether the subject is addressed in its complexity and how skills are being learned and enhanced. As with other areas of practice development, the impact of including people with direct experience of depression in later life in training programmes should not be neglected.

Professional development can also be a way to foster the confidence and capacity of front-line practitioners working in care homes, supported housing or home care. As we have suggested in the previous chapters, such staff need support and supervision if they are to sustain relationships with people who are depressed and to help prevent feelings of hopelessness developing. Working with people who are depressed takes it toll, and while supervision is not a 'cure', it can help people explore their reactions and possible frustration. For primary care organizations and social services departments, one quality indicator for organizations such as care homes may be the extent to which staff take up supervision and opportunities for training. There is much to do here; a study detecting that only two per cent of care home staff had training in the psychological care of residents (Bagley *et al.* 2000) not surprisingly observed low levels of recognition of depression among residents.

Specifically around their own commissioning we suggest that primary care organizations and local councils may find benefit in developing consensus on what 'good' local services would consist of and mark out particular areas of shortfall. Are psychological services available to older people? How big is the waiting list and how long is the waiting time? What is the referral route? Such questions can be used to inform local commissioning and service developments. Local implementation teams working to roll out the *National Service Framework for Older People* (Department of Health 2001) may have much relevant information and may have access to older people's representatives and organizations that can make these 'maps' realistic and relevant to the experiences of those who have used or tried to use services. The new GP contract may offer other opportunities, for example, in the enhanced services specification for depression. Fletcher *et al.* (2004) suggest that this provides a way to overcome key barriers such as the lack of a structured approach to developing primary care elements of local mental health services, the paucity of training and the lack of therapeutic options for people with mental health problems in primary care settings. Any such new developments need to include older people, and not just concentrate on dementia.

For social services or social work departments, we suggest that there is particular scope in exploring other elements of the 'service shortfalls' in order to contribute to this picture of local resources and areas for investment. Such data, collected if not necessarily well analyzed, through processes of assessment and care management may expose areas where practitioners think organized social support is weak in localities for depressed older people or their carers.

General practice

Within primary health care, the prescribing patterns for older people may provide data that might suggest the benefits of updating clinical practice. Prescriptions for benzodiazepines (sleeping tablets and tranquillisers), for example, may be higher than acceptable or not reviewed sufficiently often. Such recommendations relate specifically to the activities of GPs. We turn to this group of practitioners in our discussion of what elements might be further useful indicators of good practice in such services. As we have argued in previous chapters, GPs have both a role in prescribing the medical interventions that may assist in some solving or reduction of the problems of depression, but they also have a key role in referring to specialist services and working in collaboration with other networks of support.

This leads to our first point, which is to explore the interconnectedness of medical responses with psychological and social supports. Are referrals and requests appropriate, well managed and is there communication about expectations and achievements? How far do health centres make available supports for older patients with depression compared to those for other age groups? How is counselling within health centres publicized and do older people see it as accessible and relevant? Is its existence known to carers and those working with or encountering them? The evidence base for medical and psychological interventions in depression is readily available, through guidelines from the Royal College of Psychiatrists (2002) and the National Institute for Clinical Excellence (NICE) (2004).

Health centres and medical practices should have data on their identification rates of older people with depression and should have information about whether people are carers and who they are. This data may be usefully interrogated to explore if carers are receiving communications about services and networks of support, for example, alerting carers to new carers' groups in the area. This is at present hidden within the reporting requirements for payments for enhanced services, which do not distinguish between age groups when seeking data on mental health problems.

Within some primary care teams, GPs will be working with colleagues in the development of case management approaches to long-term conditions. Case management allows a more intensive, co-ordinated and personalized support service to a minority of people at high levels of risk to be planned, delivered, monitored and reviewed. Such an intensive but also holistic or 'wrap around' system may have particular benefits for those with major depression since it can be alert to changes and responsive to communication from a range of individuals in the support team. For instance, a home care worker's observations of deterioration can be quickly reported to the key worker and the situation reviewed. Case management illustrations often draw on examples of those with serious physical health problems, but they can be of equal relevance to older people with complex mental health problems that may present issues of harm or danger, and as we note earlier many people with long-term disability may be at risk of depression. As we suggest in Chapter 5, the anxiety of practitioners in working with individuals who have psychotic forms of depression may benefit from attention to channels of communication and the location of responsibility in a key worker supported by a team of other professionals.

As will be evident from the preceding chapters, we do not believe that a focus on screening within primary care services is likely to be effective on its own, partly because resources can be better used, and partly because need may be exposed without the capacity to respond. However, a clear diagnostic process is something that should be available and clinical governance process may assist in developing agreement about the most effective ways of identifying depression, distinguishing it from other issues and acknowledging its presence amid a range of other problems.

Social workers

Much of the work of social workers in mental health services for older people, and for older people generally, is similar to that of other primary care disciplines. The introduction of single assessment processes makes it more possible for information to be shared and for there to be less duplication and repetition. What can social workers do with this extra 'space'?

We suggest that social work skills in building relationships and trust may become more relevant and needed if we are to address depression. As we have shown, older people with depression may be hard to engage, may not reveal their fears and anxieties, and may be particularly afraid of the stigma of mental illness. In looking at social work services to explore their effectiveness we should therefore resist attempts to provide assessment on a one-off basis for people with depression or their carers and pay greater attention to audits of casework where there is evidence of sustained and consistent contact with those who are hard to engage, together with indicators of what to do if relapse occurs or the person's well-being deteriorates. Those older people who refuse contact may be 'known' to other agencies and service networks. Social work practitioners may have ideas of and access to community supports within neighbourhoods that can put measures in place to help with crises should they develop, and their role in supporting family members and carers of a person who does not wish to access services is potentially valuable. In assessing capacity here, local informants' knowledge of whether a social work service is responsive and accessible is likely to be an indicator of the strength of its community outreach.

Individual assessment, as we outline in Chapter 2, is potentially helpful if it has drawn out people's established coping mechanisms and experiences. This needs to be recorded in formats that are useful to colleagues and other care providers. Again, supervision can help social workers to practise or rehearse such assessments. One indicator of a good service may be social workers' use of supervision and their ability to draw on colleagues with substantial experience and knowledge, such as approved social workers (ASWs). Is such communication part of the team culture? Do ASWs see their role as providing support to colleagues in care management? How are 'cases' handled when moved from generic social work to a more specialist social work service, for instance, around compulsory assessment and treatment? Furthermore, while social workers may take on a professional advocacy role, to what extent are either local advocacy services resourced and equipped to support older people with depression? The importance of the willingness and capacity of advocacy services to work in this area will have to be developed to support older people with serious, perhaps life-threatening, depression who are detained and treated under mental health legislation.

Lastly, we consider that competence in social workers and the care team will be judged not simply by assessment but by the explicit recognition of needs and the reaching of outcomes in any care plan. In communicating the impact and extent of a person's depression to any care provider, such as a home care service or supported housing, those devising care plans will need to make sure that problems of mood, sleep and somatic symptoms can be recognized by those in day-to-day contact. Any audit of care plans for older people with depression should reveal ways in which these complexities are addressed as well as their impact with likely combinations of ill health and physical disability. Outcomes such as 'recovery' may need to be used with care, if unrealistic expectations are not to be placed on care providers. This leads to our conclusions about competency in care homes, using this as an example of support systems that include day services, short break or respite care, and home care.

Care homes

As will be evident from the above discussion, care homes play an important role in supporting older people with complex or severe disabilities, among which depression may affect their quality of life, physical health and social relationships. Staff who are trained, supported and supervised have much to offer individual residents in the way that they provide one-to-one support and respond to depression's symptoms with understanding, empathy and creativity. Those staff who are aware of the impacts of depression are likely to feel that their work is worthwhile and that they are not subject to impossible expectations. Any overview of a care home's capability in this area may find it helpful to consider staff's access to training and support. Discussions with staff may also reveal whether they feel that networks of advice are available from community nurses or specialist mental health services. How far do care home staff feel part of local networks? Is health or social services training available to staff from any setting? Is contact on a case-by-case basis or is there a system of regular contact? Is the expertise of care home staff in providing care for older people over the long term recognized in any way? How far are care home staff treated as members of the multi-disciplinary or case management team when risk assessments or decisions are made? Can care home staff or the person's key worker call for a review of medication or feel confident in suggesting that a relapse may be occurring? If we are to make use of new versions of the geriatric depression scale for nursing and residential homes (Sutcliffe *et al.* 2000), then we need to be able to help those who are found to have depression and perhaps not to rely on recognition alone producing improved outcomes (Bagley *et al.* 2000, p.447).

And finally...

This book has focused on key messages to those practitioners in health and social care who are working to support older people with depression. The main messages have been that their aim should be amelioration of problems rather than a single-minded focus on cure, that seeing depression as a disability is helpful in looking at the problem and its resolution in a new light.

We do not share the view that the growing numbers of older people will mean depression will assume epidemic proportions. We acknowledge however, that such has been the neglect of depression that many working in this area – as practitioners or carers – feel that the issue needs to be raised more forcefully. We think the area is further clouded by depression being seen so much as 'everyone's business' that it is not clear who can and should do what. In writing this book for health and social care practitioners, we hope we have avoided the temptation to push responsibility on to one sector or another. Tackling depression is a joint endeavour, with key worker roles being determined by local circumstance, often on a case-by-case basis. This means that we do not think that a service model of 'depression teams' to parallel or complement 'dementia teams' as envisaged by the *National Service Framework for Older People* (Department of Health 2001) are the way forward. Working with depression *does* need expertise and experience but such concentrations may undermine the need for almost everyone working with older people to see themselves as having a role in mental health promotion, prevention of depression and its disabilities, providing support, and identifying relapse. The experience of dementia teams as they evolve will however be important to monitor and research, to see whether such teams can make a real difference to services and mental health promotion. The extent to which they build productive relationships beyond health and social care may also be relevant to those with an interest in depression in later life.

This book has tried not to be unrealistic in assuming that depression can be cured, or even treated at times. It has tried to reflect a service and practice world where there are many pressures and insufficient resources or sources of expertise. It has been keen to reflect the complexity of supporting older people with depression and to illustrate the many, many forms this may take and the changes that are likely or possible. Supporting older people with depression is particularly challenging for those working in such services and for family members, but it is also a manageable and worthwhile task that can produce real benefit for those older people who may have suffered from depression for many years.

References

Adams, T. and Bartlett, R. (2003) 'Constructing Dementia.' In *Dementia Care* (eds) T. Adams and J. Manthorpe. London: Hodder pp.3–21.

ADSS/LGA (2003) *All Our Tomorrows: Inverting the Triangle of Care.* London: Association of Directors of Social Services/Local Government Association.

Age Concern undated *Staying well…you are worth it.* London: Age Concern.

Alexopoulos, G.S., Katz, I.R., Reynolds, C.F., Carpenter, D. and Docherty, J.P. (2001) 'The expert consensus guideline series: pharmacotherapy of depressive disorders in older patients.' *Postgrad Med Special Report.* (October) 1–86, Expert Knowledge Systems, L.L.C, Minneapolis: McGraw-Hill Healthcare Information Programs.

Anderson, I.M., Nutt, D.J. and Deakin, J.F.W. (2000) 'Evidence-based guidelines for treating depressive disorders with antidepressants: a revision of the 1993 British Association for Psychopharmacology guidelines.' *Journal of Psychopharmacology 14,* 3020.

Appleby, L. (2001) *Safety First: Five Year Report of the National Confidential Inquiry into Suicide and Homicide by People with Mental Illness.* London: Department of Health.

Arksey, H. (2003) 'Scoping the field: services for carers of people with mental health problems.' *Health and Social Care in the Community 11,* 4, 335–344.

Audit Commission (2000) *Forget Me Not: Mental Health Services for Older People.* London: Audit Commission.

Audit Commission (2004a) *Support for Carers of Older People. Independence and Well-being: The Challenge for Public Services, Report Number 5.* London: Audit Commission.

Audit Commission (2004b) *Older People – Independence and Well-being: The Challenge for Public Services.* London: Audit Commission.

Audit Commission (2004c) *Older People – A Changing Approach.* London: Audit Commission.

Audit Commission (2004d) *Supporting Frail Older People – Independence and Well-being 3.* London: Audit Commission.

Audit Commission in Wales (2004) *Developing Mental Health Services for Older People in Wales: A Follow-up to 'Losing Time'.* Cardiff: Health Wales.

Bagley, H., Cordingley, L., Burns, A., Godlove Mozley, C., Sutcliffe, C., Challis, D. and Huxley, P. (2000) 'Recognition of depression by staff in nursing and residential homes.' *Journal of Clinical Nursing 9,* 445–450.

Banerjee, S., Shamash, K., Macdonald, A. and Mann, A. (1996) 'Randomised controlled trial of effect of intervention by psychogeriatric team on depression in frail elderly people at home.' *British Medical Journal 313,* 1058–1061.

Barnes, D. (1997) *Older People with Mental Health Problems Living Alone: Anybody's Priority?* London: Social Service Inspectorate/Department of Health.

Battison, T. (2004) *Caring for Someone with Depression.* London: Age Concern.

Beekman, A.T.F., Deeg, D.J.H., Braam, A.W., Smit, J.H. and Van Tilburg, W. (1997) 'Consequences of major and minor depression in later life: a study of disability, well-being and service utilization.' *Psychiatric Medicine 27,* 6, 1397–1409.

Beekman, A.T.F., Kriegsman, D.M.W. and Deeg, D.J.H. (1995) 'The association of physical health and depressive symptoms in the older population: age and sex differences.' *Social Psychiatry Psychiatric Epidemiology 30,* 32–38.

Beinfeld, D. (1994) 'Nosology and classification.' In J.R.M. Copeland, M.T. Abou-Saleh and D.G. Blazer (eds) *Principles and Practice of Geriatric Psychiatry.* Chichester: John Wiley.

Beliappa, J. (1991) *Illness or Distress? Alternative Models of Mental Health.* London: Confederation of Indian Organisations.

Bender, M. (2003) *Explorations in Dementia.* London: Jessica Kingsley Publishers.

Biggs, S. (1992) 'Groupwork and professional attitudes to older age.' In K. Morgan (ed) *Gerontology: Responding to an Ageing Society.* London: Jessica Kingsley Publishers.

Blanchard, M.R., Waterreus, A. and Mann, A.H. (1994) 'The nature of depression among older people in inner London, and their contact with primary care.' *British Journal of Psychiatry 164,* 396–402.

Blazer, D.G. (2002) 'Self-efficacy and depression in late life: a primary prevention proposal.' *Aging and Mental Health 6,* 315–324.

Boyd, J., McKiernan, F. and Waller, G. (2000) 'Early onset and late onset depression in older adults: psychological perspectives.' *Reviews in Clinical Gerontology 10,* 2, 149–160.

Bravo, J.M. and Silverman, W.K. (2001) 'Anxiety sensitivity, anxiety and depression in older patients and their relation to hypochondriacal concerns and medical illnesses.' *Aging and Mental Health 5,* 349–357.

Bruce, M.L. and McNamara, R. (1992) 'Psychiatric status among the home bound elderly – an epidemiologic perspective.' *Journal of American Geriatric Society 40,* 6, 561–566.

Bulmer, M. (1987) *The Social Basis of Community Care.* London: Allen & Unwin.

Burkhardt, C. (1987) 'The effect of therapy on the mental health of the elderly.' *Research in Nursing and Health 10,* 277–285.

Burns, A., Jacoby, R. and Levy, R. (1990) 'Psychiatric phenomena in Alzheimer's disease. 111. Disorders of mood.' *British Journal of Psychiatry 157,* 81–86.

Cantley, C., Steven, K. and Smith, M. (2003) *Hear What I Say: Developing Dementia Advocacy Services.* Newcastle on Tyne: Dementia North.

Cattan, M. (2002) *Supporting Older People to Overcome Social Isolation and Loneliness.* London: Help the Aged.

Cattell, H.R. (1988) 'Elderly suicide in London: an analysis of coroners' inquests.' *International Journal of Geriatric Psychiatry 3,* 251–261.

Cheston, R. and Bender, M. (1999) *Understanding Dementia: The Man with the Worried Eyes.* London: Jessica Kingsley Publishers.

Cheston, R. and Jones, K. (2002) 'A place to work it all out together.' In *Dementia Topics for the Millennium and Beyond*. (ed) S. Benson. London: Hawker Publications.

Chew-Graham, C., Baldwin, R. and Burns, A. (2004) 'Treating depression in later life.' *British Medical Journal 329*, 181–182.

Churchill, R., Hunot, V., Corney, R., Knapp, M., McGuire, H., Tylee, A. and Wessely, S. (2001) 'A systematic review of controlled trials of the effectiveness and cost-effectiveness of brief psychological treatments for depression.' *Health Technology Assessment 5*, 35.

Clark, H., Dyer, S. and Horwood, J. (1998) ... *That Bit of Help... The High Value of Low Level Preventative Services for Older People*. Bristol: Policy Press.

Cohen, C.I. (1990) 'Outcome of schizophrenia in later life: an overview.' *Gerontologist 30*, 790–797.

Conaghan, S. and Davidson, K. (2002) 'Hopelessness and the anticipation of positive and negative future experiences in older parasuicidal adults.' *British Journal of Clinical Psychology 41*, 233–242.

Conn, L. and McVicker, H. (2000) 'The case of Mr Frederick Joseph McLernon: a critical examination of the findings and recommendations of the Social Services Inspectorate's Investigation Report.' *Practice 12*, 2, 22–32.

Cooke, D., McNally, L., Mulligan, K., Harrison, M. and Newman, S. (2001) 'Psychosocial interventions for caregivers of people with dementia: a systematic review.' *Aging and Mental Health 5*, 2, 120–135.

Cooper, J.K., Mungas, D., Verma, M. and Weiler, P.G. (1991) 'Psychotic symptoms in Alzheimer's disease.' *International Journal of Geriatric Psychiatry 6*, 721–726.

Craig, T.K.J. and Boardman, A.P. (1990) 'Somatisation in primary care settings.' In E. Bass (ed) *Somatisation: Physical Symptoms and Psychological Illness*. Oxford: Blackwell.

de Beurs, E., Beekman, A., Geerings, S., Deng, D., van Dyck, R. and van Tilburg, W. (2001) 'On becoming depressed or anxious in late life: similar vulnerability factors by different effects of stressful life events.' *British Journal of Psychiatry 179*, 426–431.

De Leo, D., Bruno, M.D. and Dwyer, J. (2002) 'Suicide among the elderly: the long-term impact of a telephone support and assessment intervention in northern Italy.' *British Journal of Psychiatry 181*, 226–229.

Department for Trade and Industry (1999) *Time Off for Dependants: A Short Guide*. London: Department for Trade and Industry.

Department of Health (1989) *Caring for People: Community Care in the Next Decade and Beyond*. London: Department of Health.

Department of Health (2001) *National Service Framework for Older People*. London: Department of Health.

Department of Health (2002) *National Suicide Prevention Strategy for England*. London: Department of Health.

Department of Health (2004) *The Ten Essential Shared Capabilities: A Framework for the Whole of the Mental Health Workforce*. London: Department of Health.

Department of Health (2005) *Independence, Well-being and Choice.* London: Department of Health.

Diefenbach, G.J., Stanley, M.A. and Beck, J.G. (2001) 'Worry content reported by older adults with and without generalized anxiety disorder.' *Aging and Mental Health 5,* 269–274.

Doraiswamy, P.M. (2001) 'Contemporary management of comorbid anxiety and depression in geriatric patients.' *Journal of Clinical Psychiatry 62,* 30–35.

Dwyer, S. (2003) 'The use of mental health tribunals by older people.' *Practice 15,* 3, 51–60.

Dyer, C.B., Pavlik, V., Murphy, K. and Hyman, D. (2000) 'The prevalence of depression and dementia in elder abuse and neglect.' *Journal of American Geriatrics Society 48,* 2, 205–208.

Eagles, J., Carson, D., Begg, A. and Naji, S. (2003) 'Suicide prevention: a study of patients' views.' *British Journal of Psychiatry 182,* 261–265.

Eustace, A., Denihan, A., Bruce, I., Cunningham, C., Coakley, D. and Lawlor, B.A. (2001) 'Depression in the community dwelling elderly: do clinical and sociodemographic factors influence referral to psychiatry?' *International Journal of Geriatric Psychiatry 16,* 10, 975–979.

Evans, S. and Katona, C.L.E. (1993) 'The epidemiology of depressive symptoms in elderly primary care attenders.' *Dementia 4,* 327–333.

Exton Smith, A.N., Stanton, B.R. and Windsor, A.C.M. (1976) *Nutrition of Housebound Older People.* London: King Edward's Hospital Fund.

Field, E.M., Walker, M.H. and Orrell, M.W. (2002) 'Social networks and health of older people living in sheltered housing.' *Aging and Mental Health 6,* 4, 372–386.

Firth, M., Dyer, M., Marsden, H., Savage, D. and Mohamad, H. (2004) 'Non-statutory mental health social work in primary care: a chance for renewal?' *British Journal of Social Work 34,* 2, 145–163.

Fletcher, J., Bower, P., Richards, D. and Saunders, T. (2004) *Enhanced Services Specification for Depression under the New GP Contract.* Hyde: National Institute for Mental Health in England.

Flint, A.J. (1994) 'Epidemiology and comorbidity of anxiety disorders in the elderly.' *American Journal of Psychiatry 151,* 640–49.

Flint, A.J. and Rifat, S.L. (1997) 'Anxious depression in elderly patients: response to antidepressant treatment.' *American Journal of Geriatric Psychiatry 5,* 107–15.

Floyd, M., Rice, J. and Black, S.R. (2002) 'Recurrence of posttraumatic stress disorder in late life: a cognitive aging perspective.' *Journal of Clinical Geropsychology 8,* 303–311.

Forsell, Y. and Henderson, A.S. (1998) 'Epidemiology of paranoid symptoms in an elderly population.' *British Journal of Psychiatry 172,* 429–432.

Fritsche, K., Sandholzer, H. and Werner, J. (2000) 'Psychosocial care in general practice – results of a demonstration project on quality management in psychosocial primary care.' *Psychotherapie Psychosomatik Medizinische Psycholgie 50,* 240–246.

Gallacher-Thompson, D. and de Vries, H. (1994) '"Coping with frustration" classes: development and preliminary outcomes with women who care for relatives with dementia.' *The Gerontologist 34*, 548–552.

Gallo, J.J., Rabins, P.V. and Iliffe, S. (1997) 'The "research magnificent" in later life: psychiatric epidemiology and the primary health care of older adults.' *International Journal of Psychiatry in Medicine 27*, 3, 185–204.

Garrard, J., Rolnick, S.J. and Nitz, N.M. (1998) 'Clinical detection of depression among community-based elderly people with self-reported symptoms of depression.' *Gerontology 53*, M92–M101.

Gloaguen, V., Cottraux, J., Cucherat, M. and Blackburn, M. (1998) 'A meta-analysis of the effects of cognitive therapy in depressed patients.' *Health Technology Assessment 49*, 59–72.

Goffman, E. (1963) *Stigma: Notes on the Management of Spoiled Identity*. New York: Simon & Schuster, Inc.

Goldstone, R. (1996) 'The medication role of informal carers.' *Health and Social Care in the Community 4*, 3, 150–158.

Golightly, M. (2004) *Social Work and Mental Health*. Exeter: Learning Matters.

Gove, D. (2002) 'Ethical and legal approaches to Alzheimer's disease.' In M. Warner, S. Furnish, M. Longley and B. Lawlor (eds) *Alzheimer's Disease: Policy and Practice Across Europe*. Oxford: Radcliffe, pp.27–60.

Grad, O., Clark, S., Dyregrov, K. and Andriessen, K. (2004) 'What helps and what hinders the process of surviving the suicide of somebody close?' *Crisis 25*, 3, 134–139.

Guberman, N., Nicholas, E., Nolan, M., Rembicki, D., Lundh, U. and Keefe, J. (2003) 'Impacts on practitioners of using research-based carer assessment tools: experiences from the UK, Canada and Sweden, with insights from Australia.' *Health and Social Care in the Community 11*, 4, 345–355.

Gurian, B.S., Wexler, D. and Baker, E.H. (1992) 'Late-life paranoia: possible association with early trauma and infertility.' *International Journal of Geriatric Psychiatry 7*, 277–284.

Gurland, B.J. and Cross, P.S. (1982) 'Epidemiology of psychopathology in old age.' *Psychiatric Clinics of North America 5*, 11–26.

Harris, L. (2004) 'The general practitioner's perspective.' In S. Curran and J. Wattis (eds) *Practical Management of Dementia: A Multiprofessional approach*. Oxford: Radcliffe.

Hawton, K. and Simkin, S. (2003) 'Helping people bereaved by suicide.' *British Medical Journal 327*, 177–178.

Help the Aged (2002) *Nothing Personal: Rationing Social Care for Older People*. London: Help the Aged.

Hepburn, K., Lewis, M., Wexlet Sherman, C. and Tornatore, J. (2003) 'The Savvy Caregiver Program: developing and testing a transportable family caregiver training program.' *The Gerontologist 43*, 908–915.

Hepp, U., Wittmann, L., Schnyder, U. and Michel, K. (2004) 'Psychological and psychosocial interventions after attempted suicide: an overview of treatment studies.' *Crisis 25*, 3, 108–117.

Hepple, J. and Quinton, C. (1997) 'One hundred cases of attempted suicide in the elderly.' *British Journal of Psychiatry 171*, 42–46.

Heun, R., Papassotiropoulos, A. and Ptok, U. (2000) 'Subthreshold depression and anxiety disorders in the elderly.' *European Psychiatry 15*, 3, 173–182.

Heywood, P. (2001) 'The role of primary care in the assessment, diagnosis and management of depression in older people.' In S. Curran, J.P. Wattis and S. Lynch (eds) *Practical Management of Depression in Older People.* London: Arnold.

Hinrichsen, G., Adelstein, L. and McMeniman, M. (2004) 'Expressed emotion in family members of depressed older adults.' *Aging and Mental Health 9*, 4, 353–363.

Howard, R. (2001) 'Late-onset schizophrenia and very late-onset schizophrenia-like psychosis.' *Reviews in Clinical Gerontology 11*, 337–352.

Hughes, C. (1999) 'Depression in old age.' In S. Redfern and F. Ross (eds) *Nursing Older People.* London: Churchill Livingstone.

James, I. and Sabin, N. (2002) 'Safety seeking behaviours: conceptualizing a person's reaction to the experience of cognitive confusion.' *Dementia 1*, 1, 37–46.

Jang, Y., Olivio, J., Roth, D., Haley, W. and Mittleman, M. (2004) 'Neuroticism and longitudinal change in caregiver depression: impact of a spouse-caregiver intervention programme.' *Gerontologist 44*, 3, 311–317.

Jenkins, G., Hale, R., Papanastassiou, M., Crawford, M. and Tyrer, P. (2002) 'Suicide rates 22 years after parasuicide: cohort study.' *British Medical Journal 325*, 1155.

Jorm, A.F. (2000) 'Mental health literacy.' *British Medical Journal 177*, 396–401.

Joseph Rowntree Foundation (1999) *Developing a Preventive Approach with Older People.* York: Joseph Rowntree Foundation.

Judd, L.L., Akiskal, H.S., Maser, J.D., Zeller, P.J., Endicott, J., Coryell, W., Paulus, M.P., Kunovac, J.L., Leon, A.C., Mueller, T.J., Rice, J.A. and Keller, M.B. (1998) 'A prospective 12-year study of subsyndromal and syndromal depressive symptoms in unipolar major depressive disorders.' *Archives of General Psychiatry 55*, 694–700.

Katona, C. (1994) *Depression in Old Age.* Chichester: Wiley.

Katona, C.L.E. (1989) 'The epidemiology and natural history of depression in old age.' In K. Ghose (ed) *Antidepressants for Elderly People.* London: Chapman & Hall.

Katona, C., Freeling, P., Hinchcliffe, K., Blanchard, M. and Wright, A. (1995) 'Recognition and management of depression in late life in general practice: consensus statement.' *Primary Care Psychiatry 1*, 107–113.

Kennedy, G.L., Kelman, H.R. and Thomas, C. (1990) 'The emergence of depressive symptoms in late life: the importance of declining health and increasing disability.' *Journal of Community Health 15*, 93–104.

Kirby, M., Bruce, I., Coakley, D. and Lawlor, B.A. (1999) 'Dysthymia among the community-dwelling elderly.' *International Journal of Geriatric Psychiatry 14*, 6, 440–445.

Kirby, M., Denihan, A., Bruce, I., Radic, A., Coakley, D. and Lawlor, B.A. (1999) 'Benzodiazepine use among the elderly in the community.' *International Journal of Geriatric Psychiatry 14*, 280–284.

Koffman, J. and Higginson, I. (2003) 'Fit to care? A comparison of informal caregivers of first-generation Black Caribbeans and White dependents with advanced progressive disease in the UK.' *Health and Social Care in the Community 11*, 6, 528–536.

Kramer, M., German, P.S. and Anthony, J.C. (1985) 'Patterns of mental disorder among the elderly residents of Eastern Baltimore.' *Journal of American Geriatric Society 33*, 236–245.

Krasucki, C., Ryan, P., Ertan, T., Howard, R., Lindesay, J. and Mann, A. (1999) 'The FEAR: A rapid screening instrument for generalized anxiety in elderly primary care attenders.' *International Journal of Geriatric Psychiatry 14*, 60–68.

Lacro, J.P., Harris, M.J. and Jeste, D.V. (1995) 'Late life psychosis.' In E. Murphy and G. Alexopoulos (eds) *Geriatric Psychiatry: Key Research Topics for Clinicians.* Chichester: John Wiley.

Ladyman, S. (2004) *Speech to the Association of Directors of Social Services Spring Seminar* www.adss.org.uk/events/ladyman.shtml

Leason, K. (2004) 'A cure for depression?' *Community Care 2*, December, 44–45.

Lebowitz, B.D., Pearson, J.L. and Schneider, L.S. (1997) 'Diagnosis and treatment of depression in late life.' *Journal of the American Medical Association 278*, 1186–1190.

Leff, J. (2001) *The Unbalanced Mind.* London: Wiedenfeld and Nicholson.

Lenze, E.J., Mulsant, B.H. and Shear, M.K. (2000) 'Comorbid anxiety disorders in depressed elderly patients.' *American Journal of Psychiatry 157*, 722–728.

Lenze, E.J., Mulsant, B.H., Shear, M.K., Alexopoulos, G.S., Frank, E. and Reynolds, C.E. (2001) 'Co-morbidity of depression and anxiety disorders in later life.' *Depression and Anxiety 14*, 86–93.

Lenze, E.J., Rogers, J.C., Martire, L.M., Mulsant, B.H., Rollman, B.L., Dew, M.A., Schulz, R. and Reynolds, C.F. (2001) 'The association of late-life depression and anxiety with physical disability – a review of the literature and prospects for future research.' *American Journal of Geriatric Psychiatry 9*, 2, 113–135.

Lindesay, J. (1997) 'Phobic disorders and fear of crime in the elderly.' *Aging and Mental Health 1*, 81–86.

Lindesay, J., Briggs, S.K. and Murphy, E. (1989) 'The Guy's/Age Concern survey prevalence rates of cognitive impairment, depression and anxiety in an urban elderly community.' *British Journal of Psychiatry 155*, 377–389.

Livingston, G., Manela, M. and Katona, C. (1996) 'Depression and other psychiatric morbidity in carers of elderly people living at home.' *British Medical Journal 312*, 153–156.

Lyness, J.M., Caine, E.D., King, D.A., Cox, C. and Yoediono, Z. (1999) 'Psychiatric disorders in older primary care patients.' *Journal of General Internal Medicine 14*, 4, 249–254.

MacDonald, A.J.D. (1986) 'Do general practitioners miss depression in elderly patients?' *British Medical Journal 292*, 1365–1367.

Maidment, R., Livingston, G. and Katona, C. (2002) '"Just keep taking the tablets": adherence to anti-depressant treatment in older people in primary care.' *International Journal of Geriatric Psychiatry 17*, 8, 752–757.

Mann, A., Schneider, J., Moxley, C., Levin, E., Blizard, R., Netten, A., Egelstaff, R. and Abbey, A. (2000) 'Depression and the response of residential homes to physical health needs.' *International Journal of Geriatric Psychiatry 15*, 12, 1105–1112.

Manthorpe, J., Caan, W. and Stanley, N. (2001) 'Managers' and practitioners' experiences of depression: a unifying phenomenon?' *MCC: Building Knowledge for Integrated Care 10*, 4, 27–30.

Marriott, A., Donaldson, C., Turner, N. and Burns, A. (2000) 'Effectiveness of cognitive-behavioural family intervention in reducing the burden of care in carers of patients with Alzheimer's disease.' *British Journal of Psychiatry 176*, 557–562.

Marshall, M. (2001) 'The challenge of looking after people with dementia.' *British Medical Journal 323*, 410–411.

Mather, A., Rodriguez, C., Guthrie, M., McHarg, A., Reid, I. and McMurdo, M. (2002) 'Effects of exercise on depressive symptoms in older adults with poorly responsive depressive disorder.' *British Journal of Psychiatry 180*, 411–415.

McCabe, R., Heath, C., Burns, T. and Priebe, S. (2002) 'Engagement of patients with psychosis in the consultation: conversation analytic study.' *British Medical Journal 325*, 1148–1151.

McCall, W.V., Dunn, A. and Rosenquist, P.B. (2004) 'Quality of life and function after electroconvulsive therapy.' *British Journal of Psychiatry 185*, 405–409.

McCusker, J., Cole, M., Keller, E., Bellavance, F. and Berard, A. (1998) 'Effectiveness of treatments of depression in older ambulatory patients.' *Archives of Internal Medicine 158*, 705–712.

McGlashlan, T.H. (1986) 'Predictors of shorter-, medium- and longer-term outcomes in schizophrenia.' *American Journal of Psychiatry 143*, 50–55.

McLaughlin, E. (1994) 'Legacies of caring: the experience and circumstances of ex-carers.' *Health and Social Care in the Community 2*, 4, 241–254.

McLean, J., Platt, S. and Woodhouse, A. (2004) *Suicide and Suicidal Behaviour: Establishing the Territory for a Series of Research Reviews.* Edinburgh: Scottish Executive.

McWilliam, C.L., Stewart, M. and Brown, J.B. (1999) 'Home-based health promotion for chronically ill older people: results of a randomized controlled trial of a critical reflection approach.' *Health Promotion International 14*, 217–241.

Menec, V. (2003) 'The relation between everyday activities and successful ageing: a 6-year longitudinal study.' *Journal of Gerontological and Scientific Social Science 58,* S74–82.

Miller, E., Berrios, G. and Politynska, B. (1996) 'Caring for someone with Parkinson's disease: factors that contribute to distress.' *British Journal of Clinical Psychology 33,* 333–344.

Milne, A., Hatzidimitriadou, E., Chryssanthopoulou, C. and Owen, T. (2001) *Caring in Later Life: Reviewing the Role of Older Carers.* London: Help the Aged.

Minardi, H. and Blanchard, M. (2004) 'Older people with depression: pilot study.' *Journal of Advanced Nursing 46,* 1, 23–32.

Mitchell, F. (1996) 'Carer support groups: the effects of organizational factors on the character of groups.' *Health and Social Care in the Community 4,* 2, 113–121.

Mofic, H.S. and Paykel, E.S. (1975) 'Depression in medical in-patients.' *British Journal of Psychiatry 126,* 346–353.

Montano, C.B. (1999) 'Primary care issues related to the treatment of depression in elderly patients.' *Journal of Clinical Psychiatry 60,* 45–51.

Moxon, S., Lyne, K., Sinclair, I., Young, P. and Kirk, C. (2001) 'Mental health in residential homes: a role for care staff.' *Ageing and Society 21,* 71–94.

Mulley, G. (2001) 'Depression in physically ill older people.' In S. Curran, J. Wattis and S. Lynch (eds) *Practical Management of Depression in Older People.* London: Arnold.

Murphy, E. (1983) 'The prognosis of depression in old age.' *British Journal of Psychiatry 142,* 111–119.

Murphy, E. (1988) 'Prevention of depression and suicide.' In B. Gearing, M. Johnson and T. Heller (eds) *Mental Health Problems in Old Age.* Chichester: Wiley.

Murray, J., Manela, M., Shuttleworth, A. and Livingston, G. (1997) 'Caring for an older spouse with a psychiatric illness.' *Aging and Mental Health 1,* 3, 256–261.

National Institute for Clinical Excellence (2004) *Depression: Management of Clinical Depression in Primary and Secondary Care: Clinical Guideline 23.* London: NICE.

National Institute for Mental Health England (NIMHE) (2004) *Celebrating Our Cultures: Guidelines for Mental Health Promotion with Black and Minority Ethnic Communities.* London: Mentality/National Institute for Mental Health England.

Newton, J. (1988) *Preventing Mental Illness.* London: Routledge.

Nolan, J. (2001) 'Community Care.' In M. Nolan, S. Davies and G. Grant (eds) *Working with Older People and their Families: Key Issues in Policy and Practice.* Buckingham: Open University Press.

Nolan, M. and Grant, G. (1992) *Regular Respite: An Evaluation of a Hospital Rota Bed Scheme for Elderly people.* London: Age Concern.

Nolan, M. and Keady, J. (2001) 'Working with carers.' In C. Cantley (ed) *A Handbook of Dementia Care.* Buckingham: Open University Press.

Nolan, M., Grant, G. and Keady, J. (1996) *Understanding Family Care.* Buckingham: Open University Press.

Nolan, M., Keady, J. and Grant, G. (1995) 'CAMI: a basis for assessment and support with family carers.' *British Journal of Nursing 4,* 14, 822–826.

Nolan, P., Badger, F. and Dunn, L. (1999) 'Brainstorming the role of mental health nursing.' *Nursing Times 17*, 4, 52–54.

Nowers, A. (1993) 'Deliberate self harm in the elderly: a survey of one London Borough.' *International Journal of Geriatric Psychiatry 6*, 7, 609–614.

Nurock, S. (2002) 'GPs: we need you!' In S. Benson (ed) *Dementia Topics for the Millennium and Beyond.* London: Hawker Publications.

O'Connell, H., Chin, A-V., Cunningham, C. and Lawlor, B. (2004) 'Recent developments in suicide in older people.' *British Medical Journal 329*, 895–899.

Olafsdottir, M., Marcusson, J. and Skoog, I. (2001) 'Mental disorders among elderly people in primary care: the Linkoping study.' *Acta Psychiatrica Scandinavia 104*, 1, 12–18.

Ormel, J., Rijsdijk, F.V., Sullivan, M., van Sonderen, E. and Kempen, G.I.J.M. (2002) 'Temporal and reciprocal relationship between IADL/ADL disability and depressive symptoms in late life.' *Gerontology 57*, 4, 338–347.

Pannell, J., Morbey, H. and Means, R. (2002) *Surviving at the Margins: Older Homeless People and the Organisations that Support Them.* London: Help the Aged.

Patmore, C. (2002) 'Morale and quality of life among frail older users of community care: key issues for the success of community care.' *Quality in Ageing 3*, 22–29.

Postle, K. (2001) 'The social work side is disappearing: I guess it started with us being called care managers.' *Practice 13*, 1, 13–26.

Préville, M., Côté, G., Boyer, R. and Hébert, R. (2004) 'Detection of depression and anxiety by home care nurses.' *Aging and Mental Health 8*, 5, 400–409.

Priest, R., Vize, C. and Roberts, A. (1996) 'Lay people's attitudes to treatment of depression: results of opinion poll for Defeat Depression Campaign just before its launch.' *British Medical Journal 313*, 858–859.

Quam, H. and Arboleda-Florez, J. (1997) 'Elderly suicide in Alberta: difference by gender.' *Canadian Journal of Psychiatry 5*, 55–65.

Quilgars, D. (2000) *Low Intensity Support Services: A Systematic Literature Review.* Bristol: Policy Press.

Redfield Jamison, K. (2000) *Night Falls Fast.* London: Picador.

Rogers, H. (2000) 'Breaking the ice: developing strategies for collaborative working with carers of older people with mental health problems.' In H. Kemshall and R. Littlechild (eds) *User Involvement and Participation in Social Care.* London: Jessica Kingsley Publishers.

Routasalo, P. and Pitkala, K. (2003) 'Loneliness among older people.' *Reviews in Clinical Gerontology 13*, 4, 303–312.

Rowe, D. (2003) *Depression: The Way Out of Your Prison.* London: Routledge.

Royal College of Psychiatrists (2002) *Guidelines for the Assessment and Management of Later Life Depression in Primary Care.* London: Royal College of Psychiatrists.

Royal College of Psychiatrists (2004) *Carers and Confidentiality in Mental Health: Issues Involved in Information-sharing.* London: Royal College of Psychiatrists.

Rutz, W., von Knorring, L., Walinder, J. and Wisedt, B. (1989) 'Frequency of suicide in Gotland after systematic postgraduate education of general practitioners.' *Acta Psychiatrica Scandinavia 80*, 151–154.

Salib, E. and Green, L. (2003) 'Gender and elderly suicide: analysis of coroners' inquests of 200 cases of elderly suicide in Cheshire 1989–2001.' *International Journal of Geriatric Psychiatry 18*, 1082–1087.

Scharf, T., Phillipson, C., Smith, A. and Kingston, P. (2002) *Growing Older in Socially Deprived Areas.* London: Help the Aged.

Schulz, R., Newsom, J., Fleissner, K., deCamp, A. and Nieboer, A. (1997) 'The effects of bereavement after family caregiving.' *Aging and Mental Health 1*, 3, 269–283.

Scottish Executive (2003) *National Programme to Improve Mental Health and Well-being: Action Plan 2003–2006.* Edinburgh: Scottish Executive.

Seymour, L. and Gale, E. (2004) *Literature and Policy Review for the Joint Inquiry into Mental Health and Well-being in Later Life.* London: Mentality.

Shah, R., Uren, Z. and Baker, A. (2002) 'Trends in suicide from drug overdose in the elderly in England and Wales 1993–1999.' *International Journal of Geriatric Psychiatry 17*, 416–421.

Sharma, V.K. and Copeland, J.R.M. (1989) 'Presentation and assessment of depression in old age.' In K. Ghose (ed) *Antidepressants for Elderly People.* London: Chapman & Hall.

Shaw, C., Creed, F., Tomenson, B., Riste, L., Cruikshank, J. and Rait, G. (1999) 'Prevalence of anxiety and depression illness help seeking behaviour in African Caribbeans and white Europeans: two phase general populations survey.' *British Medical Journal 318*, 302–306.

Sheehan, B. and Banerjee, S. (1999) 'Review: Somatization in the elderly.' *International Journal of Geriatric Psychiatry 14*, 1044–1049.

Sidorenko, A. and Walker, A. (2004) 'The Madrid International Plan of Action on Ageing: from conception to completion.' *Ageing and Society 24*, 2, 147–166.

Snowden, J. (2001) 'Suicide in late life.' *Reviews in Clinical Gerontology 11*, 253–360.

Snyder, L., Quayhagen, M., Shepherd, S. and Bower, D. (1995) 'Supportive seminar groups: an intervention for early stage dementia patients.' *The Gerontologist 35*, 5, 691–695.

Social Care Institute for Excellence (2004) *Assessing Mental Health Needs of Older People.* London: Social Care Institute for Excellence.

Social Services Inspectorate (1998) *Community Care: From Policy to Practice. The Case of Mr Frederick Joseph McLernon (deceased).* Belfast: HMSO.

Styron, W. (1996) 'Darkness visible.' In S. Dunn, B. Morrison and M. Roberts (eds) *Mind Readings: Writers' Journey Through Mental States.* London: Minerva.

Sutcliffe, C., Cordingley, L., Burns, A., Godlove Mozley, C., Bagley, H., Huxley, P. and Challis, D. (2000) 'A new version of the geriatric depression scale for nursing and residential home populations: the geriatric depression scale (residential) (GDS12-R).' *International Psychogeriatrics 12*, 2, 173–181.

Teri, L. and Logsdon, R. (1991) 'Identifying pleasant activities for Alzheimer's patients: the Pleasant Events Schedule AD.' *The Gerontologist 31*, 124–127.

Teri, L., Logsdon, R., Uomoto, J. and McCurry, S. (1997) 'Behavioural treatment of depression in dementia patients; a controlled clinical trial.' *Journal of Gerontology Series B, Psychology and Social Sciences 552B,* 159–166.

Teri, L. and Reifler, B. (1997) 'Disease and dementia.' In L. Carstensen and B. Edelstein (eds) *Handbook of Clinical Gerontology.* New York; Raven Press.

Teri, L., Ferretti, L., Gibbons, L., Logsdon, R., McCurry, S., Kukull, W., McCormick, W., Bowen, J. and Larson, E. (1999) 'Anxiety of Alzheimer's disease: prevalence, and comorbidity.' *Journal of Gerontology 54,* 7, M348–352.

Twigg, J. (2000) *Bathing – The Body and Community Care.* London: Routledge.

Twigg, J. and Atkin, K. (1994) *Carers Perceived.* Buckingham: Open University Press.

Ustün, T. and Kessler, R. (2002) 'Global burden of depressive disorders: the issue of duration.' *British Journal of Psychiatry 181,* 181–183.

Van Willigen, M. (2000) 'Differential benefits of volunteering across the life course.' *Journal of Gerontological Behavioral and Social Science 55,* (5), S308–318.

Walker, S. and Beckett, C. (2003) *Social Work Assessment and Intervention.* Lyme Regis: Russell House Publishing.

Warr, P., Butcher, V. and Robertson, I. (2004) 'Activity and psychological well-being in older people.' *Aging and Mental Health 8,* 2, 172–183.

Watts, S.C., Bhutani, G.E., Stout, I.H., Ducker, G.M., Cleator, R.J., McGarry, J. and Day, M. (2002) 'Mental health in older recipients of primary care services; is depression the key issue? Identification, treatment and the general practitioner.' *International Journal of Geriatric Psychiatry 17,* 5, 427–437.

Weiner, M. (2004) 'Management of emotional and behavioural symptoms in Alzheimer's disease.' In R. Rocher and F. Rocher (eds) *Alzheimer's Disease: A Physician's Guide to Practical Management.* New Jersey: Human Press.

Weiss, K.J. (1996) 'Optimal management of anxiety in older patients.' *Drugs and Aging 9,* 191–201.

Wetherell, J.L. (1998) 'Treatment of anxiety in older adults.' *Psychotherapy 35,* 444–458.

Wistow, G. (2004) *The New Vision for Adult Social Care: Responses to a Survey Conducted by the Social Care Institute for Excellence.* London: Social Care Institute for Excellence.

Wolpert, L. (1999) *Malignant Sadness: The Anatomy of Depression.* London: Faber and Faber.

World Psychiatric Association (WPA) (1999) *WPA International Committee for Prevention and Treatment of Depression Depressive Disorders in Older Persons.* New York: NCM Publishers. www.Wpanet.org/sectorial/edu4.html

Subject Index

Author Index